LETTER TO ROBIN

Dowsing Insights & Tested Protocols

Walt Woods

Edited by:

Nina Gee

William Gee

&

Joan Nathenson

AMERICAN SOCIETY OF DOWSERS

ISBN: 979-8-9875527-0-4 (Paperback)

Cover Art and Book Design by Nina Gee

MANY THANKS

To my loving wife Joyce for her
infinite patience and excellent
spelling ability. To Angela, Boyd,
Carmen, Cynthia, Jeanne, Joline,
Linda, Nicolas, Robin and Tony
for their editing suggestions.
Special thanks to Lea Kachadorian,
Bob Sird, Kay Lamm, Mardi
Gieseler, Penn Bell, Nicolas
Finck, Mike Doney, and
to the many other dowsers who shared
their wisdom, ideas, experiences
and understanding to help make
this book possible.

Walt Woods

Letter to Robin

Table of Contents

Editor's Note: How this Book Came to Be

In 2011, the dowsing world lost one of its most beloved influencers and teachers. For years, Walt Woods was an inspiration for future dowsers while also serving as President of the American Society of Dowsers (ASD) for several years.

Letter to Robin started out as a personal response to a young woman named Robin, who wrote to the ASD asking for help in learning to dowse. Soon the contents of this letter became a short booklet containing all the basic tips and tricks that Walt had discovered and developed as he taught beginning dowsers. Eventually, it became the go-to resource for dowsing teachers worldwide. It was translated into several different languages and distributed free of charge to anyone who wanted to download it from the internet.

In 2022, at the request of Walt's family, the American Society of Dowsers purchased copyrights to all of Walt's published works relating to information in *Letter to Robin*, including some of his lesser-known writing on more advanced dowsing techniques he was developing.

The vision for this current publication was to create a textbook that would be an easy-to-read and easy-to-use resource for the beginning dowser, light enough to be approachable, but containing enough useful information that even the most advanced dowser would benefit from reading it. The editorial team, in consultation with the ASD Board of Trustees, decided that instead of simply recreating or recopying the original text, we would edit and combine all of Walt's published works together in a single volume.

In addition to this book, we have also created a companion journal that not only contains all the dowsing charts that you can lay flat on any surface, but also lots of blank pages for you to keep track of your daily dowsing practice. The companion journal is available in both print and in digital journal format that can be used on any tablet device!

Letter to Robin has been an absolute pleasure for us to develop. We hope you love it as much as we loved putting it together for you!

Nina, Bill & Joan
April 9, 2023

Introduction to the 10th Revision of *Letter to Robin*

Walt Woods

A young woman named Robin was having the same problems that many beginning dowsers have - trouble with accuracy and repeatability. Wisely, she wrote to the American Society of Dowsers asking for help. When the Society sent her the names of ten dowsers, I was privileged to be one of them. Robin then sent a letter to each one and received informative letters from all of us. While I had recognized the need for a written reference guidelines for new dowsers for some time, it was this letter that inspired me to start developing it. With suggestions from many dowsers, *Letter to Robin* is now in its tenth revision with subsequent minor revisions for clarity.[1]

Over a period of ten years, starting in 1980, I had developed a Multipurpose Dowsing Chart with an accompanying booklet explaining how to use it. Starting as one page, it eventually grew through 26 revisions to eight pages. After these updates were given away at many dowsing meetings, I received

---

[1] Editor's note: This work is a compilation of several booklets written by Walt Woods that have been reorganized and edited for clarity and readability. Therefore, we can technically refer to it as an eleventh edition, although it is the first edition under the copyright of The American Society of Dowsers.

new information and suggestions from many dowsers, which stimulated yet more improvements.

Eventually, the Chart evolved into a Multipurpose Dowsing System that was so in-depth that beginning dowsers had trouble understanding it. Then I realized the need for a simple, easy-to-understand, how-to-learn-to-dowse booklet. It needed to include instructions for using the pendulum, programming (establishing parameters and conditions for dowsing) and how to ask good dowsing questions. Even though dowsers successfully use many different devices and methods, there appears to be an underlying basic system at work. Skilled dowsers usually specialize and may add many refinements to the basic systems.[2]

This book includes content from the following booklets:

- Letter to Robin

- Companion to Letter to Robin

- Foundation Programs

- Food and Other Concerns

- Personal Dowsing

- Advanced Dowsing Research

---

[2] Editor's Note: While this current edition of *Letter to Robin* text can be used as the primary text for a basic course on dowsing, it can also be used as the foundation for discussions by experienced dowsers as it contains information that even the most skilled dowsers may appreciate or find useful. It can be used in a classroom or as a supplement to solitary study. Our hope is that it conveys the experience, wit, and humor of one of the most respected and sought-after dowsers in our Society.

Who Can Dowse?

Let's first look at the abilities of our Subconscious mind. Have you ever had the experience of staring at a person, then have them immediately turn and look right at you? Have you had the phone ring and you somehow knew it was Uncle Joe even though you hadn't thought of him in a long time, and you were right? Have you ever had a very good idea just pop into your mind seemingly out of nowhere? Does your body suddenly react like taking your foot off the accelerator and putting it on the break almost before you are aware of impending danger? How does a mother know that her child is in trouble even though they may not be nearby? These and many other similar experiences have happened to almost everyone. As you can see, the Subconscious, or some aspect of it, has excellent sensing and reacting abilities to our internal states, nearby situations, or distant occurrences.

Can you train or program your Subconscious, or some aspect of it, to use many types of tools or devices? Of course! Dowsing uses the same method that you used to train, or program, your Subconscious to automatically write your name, type, or play an instrument. You will be simply programming your Subconscious to express its available information with some type of indicating method or device. Basic dowsing is quick and easy to learn. While like most procedures, it will take practice and experience to be and stay good at it, you will be surprised how easy it is to get started!

How Do I Get Started?

Start the same way you programmed (or trained) your body to write your name, type, or play a musical instrument. When you were learning, you deliberately practiced moving your fingers with intent until you established ideomotor reactions.[3] If you make the pendulum[4] swing to YES on a chart over and over again, telling it this is YES, soon your Subconscious will be able to swing the pendulum by itself with just a question and intent on your part. Then, if you do this for NO and "Ready for Question", the Subconscious now has a way of directly communicating with you. *See "YES/NO Chart" in Appendix A: The Charts.* (page 145)

Suggestions for Using "Letter to Robin"

1. Glance through the index, or the entire book just to get a feeling for what it includes.

---

[3] Measurable electrical signals that move the muscles. These can be measured with a myograph instrument on a dowser when they are dowsing.

[4] A pendulum is a weight suspended on a string which can swing freely from a resting vertical position.

2. Next, train your Subconscious to move the pendulum in the same way you originally trained your Subconscious to write your name. Place the *"YES/NO Chart"* in front of you, preferably on a flat surface, from *Appendix A: The Charts*. (page 145) Take your pendulum in your dominant hand and hold it by the chain or string with your thumb and index finger, about 2-3 inches up from the weight. Deliberately make your fingers swing the pendulum to YES until it can do this motion by itself. Tell your Subconscious this represents a YES answer. This swing can become just as automatically subconsciously controlled as making the letters in your name. Do the same for NO and Ready for Question.

3. Once your Subconscious is trained (or programmed) to move the pendulum to YES, NO, and Ready for Question, it is time to instruct, or program your Subconscious on how, what, and when, to respond. The Subconscious does not know what you want until you tell it. The same way that your Subconscious did not know how you wanted it to write your name until you programmed it. One way to inform your Subconscious of what you want is to install the *"Primary Program"* and the *"May I, Can I, Should I? Program"* found later in this text. Use the three-step instructions provided for you. It helps if you read the programs aloud with your pendulum swinging to YES and positioned a little to the side, but where you can still see it.

4. Now you are ready to use dowsing to obtain information. To do this you should pick an area of interest and install its program. As many people seem to be attracted to researching their personal being, we will start there. Your Dowsing System must have agreed to accept the Program by going to YES and staying on YES while you read in the Program.

5. To install this program, start by reading the beginning of *"Conditions Program"* (page 106) and continue to the bottom of the section where it says **"End of Program. Thank you."**

Note: With the Conditions Program, your Dowsing System will be using a reference or comparison person of your age and peer group. This comparison person will be indicated by the pendulum swinging vertically to the "Bal" (Balanced) position. When you ask about yourself, your eventual goal would likely be to have the pendulum indicate a +10 on the beneficial side, meaning best possible, rather than average.

6. To use *"100 Interesting Areas to Explore"*, (page 95) start by having your pendulum swinging to "Ready for Question". Next, ask the first question, then question 2. If your pendulum swings to the negative side of the chart you might want to take notice. This would suggest that you have an area which is not as good as the reference person.

7. If you happen get a negative reading you might wish to look at the section on *"Possible Corrections to Detrimental Situations"*,(page 119) which will give you some suggestions on how to ask your Subconscious to possibly adjust these negative energies.

8. If you wish to know what the negative reading is referring to, simply refer to the areas of the *"Conditions List"* on page 123, to indicate the level of each one. To do this more quickly, you might ask the system to indicate which section number, 1 through 4 to look at. This will speed up your search.

9. To learn more about when you can trust your dowsing, go to page 54. Be sure to read the *"Caution"* footnote on the bottom of page 75.

10. Other Programs throughout *Letter to Robin* are fun to work with and we will approach them in the same way. They all work well with the *Multipurpose Chart* in the *Appendix: The Charts* section of this book beginning on page 145.

A Word of Warning: Go slowly, be careful, and work with experienced dowsers when it involves other people or their money. In time, and with practice, you will become an accomplished dowser who will be very helpful to yourself and others.

Some Word Definitions Used Throughout This Book

The following words have different meanings for different persons and different groups of people at different times. In this book, however, the following definitions apply.

Dowsing System: I use these words to express an idea, because there seem to be many aspects to what is going on when we dowse, although we do not clearly understand them all at this time. It is the physical aspect of programming or training the Subconscious to express itself automatically, as well as when specifically, being requested to demonstrate in lab tests. Even though much of the information seems to come from (or through) the Subconscious, there are most likely many other contributing sources. So, for lack of better words, I call this the Dowsing System, or simply, The System.

Noxious Energies: Any form of energy, condition, zone, or situation that is, or could adversely affect any aspect of my personal being in a harmful, disrupting, or interfering way, by exceeding my healing and defensive mechanisms.

Subconscious: Being Conscious is when you are awake and aware, but it probably uses less than one thousandth of your total sensing system. The Subconscious is all the other awareness and sensing activities your being utilizes. The Subconscious can sense inside objects or living beings or situations at a great distance as well as nearby, and there are thousands of other reactions going on all the time. Often by using dowsing or other response systems, some interesting aspect of this sensing and other information can be encouraged to come through to your conscious awareness.

Superconscious and Higher Self: These areas may in some way be related on a spiritual level. These may also be areas that make us feel alive and may pop ideas into our heads seemingly out of nowhere. Some people seem to relate this to some aspect of the Creative Force, etc. How you describe this reality is your choice.

Spirit Guides or Guardian Angels: Many people believe that there are Entities or Spiritual Beings that help guide us, particularly in our spiritual growth. They seem to be able to contact us on a very subtle level (possibly even through our dowsing) by influencing some aspects of the responding abilities of our Subconscious.

Entities: For our purposes let us assume that an Entity is not a negative being, but is simply you, me, or perhaps some other being without a physical body. In this form, it is often referred to as an Astral or Spiritual Body. They are fully aware, alert, and may still have their previous intents and attitudes but are invisible to most humans. They can usually see us but not very well. At this different frequency, they can walk right through us and the walls. They can stay on the earth plane, sometimes near their families; perhaps join their family or a religious group on other planes; or perhaps go through a tunnel toward the light or whatever you wish to believe.

Walt Woods

Dowsing Basics

I received a thoughtful letter from "Robin" asking some interesting questions about dowsing. The following is a reconstruction of my reply.

Dear Robin,

First, thank you for your letter of inquiry. You have raised some very interesting questions, which I will attempt to answer as best as I can. You stated that your dowsing wasn't working very well, and that you didn't feel you could trust it. You were curious if one dowsing tool was better than another. You asked if I could give you some ideas on how to improve your dowsing. You also said that you had heard that the wording of questions asked while dowsing was very important. I hope I can be of some help. Please let me suggest some ideas for your consideration.

Some Useful Definitions

1. **Dowsing** (*also referred to as Water Witching, Divining, Questing, Doodle Bugging, etc.*) is the ancient art of finding water, minerals and other objects

that seem to have a natural magnetic, electromagnetic, or other unknown energy. It is a means by which we can tap into our Superconscious, Subconscious, Spirit Guides, etc., for information and action. This is accompanied by some method for detecting this information. A certain visual stimulus (i.e. violence, a couple in love, etc.) may cause an emotional response, a feeling in your stomach, and probably other unnoticed Subconscious reactions. It may be that similar types of subtle unnoticed Subconscious reactions, possibly from water or other sources, may give a subconsciously controlled response by means of numerous types of dowsing devices. The body seems to detect these energies with its built-in, laboratory-demonstrable sensors, that are no more mysterious than seeing, hearing or feeling, and seem to be natural to all of us. As it is with music, many persons can develop degrees of dowsing skill with training and practice. Every culture in the world, even as far back as cave dwellers who left us their art before written language was invented, has had some type of dowsing.

2. A **Dowsing device** seems to be simply a connector between our sensing system and our conscious mind. We live in a fascinating world.

3. **Dowsing clubs** are organizations formed to enable dowsers to share experiences, successes, or failures; gather information about dowsing phenomena; and learn to apply it wisely. Dowsing draws together people with open and searching minds who have discovered that we are sensitive to and respond to many subtle energies.

How Dowsing Works

The Mind

Let's start with the possible involvement of the mind, which apparently needs to be busy. You need to talk and listen when you are dowsing. The mind also needs to feel that it understands what is going on. You can satisfy these two needs, being busy and understanding, in several ways. First, if you use a dowsing instrument, then your mind is busy watching the tool work. There is motion, intrigue, expectation, and anticipation, all of which your mind enjoys. Next, if your mind has a plausible explanation of what is going on, it doesn't become frustrated and doubtful. You need is at least a partial, rational, explanation of how dowsing works.[5]

---

[5] Editor's note: The author believed that "the mind" did not exist within the human brain, but it exists as an information field outside of the brain that humans can access. This is an idea that is supported by Carl Jung's theory of the "collective unconscious", and more recently by Dr. Daniel Siegel, who is a Clinical Professor of Psychiatry at the Mindful Awareness Research Center at UCLA.

Letter to Robin

The Human Electromagnetic Sensory System

You can find information about our sensory systems scattered throughout many scientific and metaphysical books and articles. In a scientific article from 1989, a neurophysiologist at the Veteran's Association Medical Center in Loma Linda, California, indicated that they were observing effects from electric fields only one millionth as strong as those formerly considered threshold levels in humans.[6] This was news to most scientists, yet dowsers already knew that if you pass electricity through the ground, you could easily pick up the resulting electromagnetic energies. This experiment had been done in the past at many dowsing conventions.[7]

In our bodies, we have three sensors that can pick up this electromagnetic information. One is on the pituitary gland, and one on each adrenal gland. Having three points, the Subconscious can determine both distance and direction of an electromagnetic source. This is probably done in a similar way that the Subconscious uses data from two eyes to determine distance.

---

[6] Source: 1989, Nair, Morgan, et al; "Biological Effects of Power Frequency Electric and Magnetic Fields", Carnegie Mellon University.
https://citeseerx.ist.psu.edu/document?repid=rep1&type=pdf&doi=8626ee3aa9d159e9eed4b0befda41aacdf d4403b
[7] Bird, The Divining Hand. Whitford Press, 1993. This newly revised book is an excellent text about dowsing and its history. It is not a "how-to-dowse" book.

Passing Electricity Through the Ground

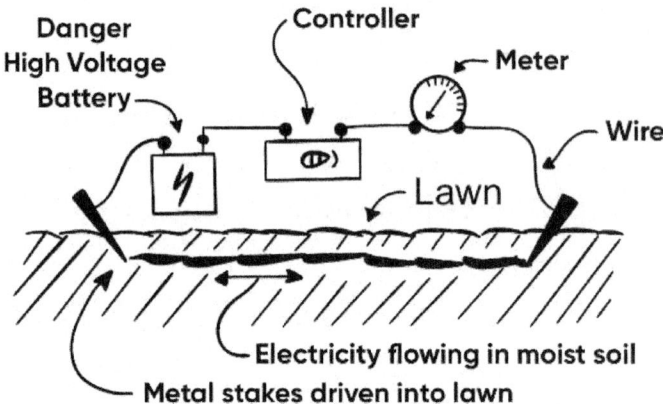

Water and Electricity

A simple science fair experiment can show that moving water can cause electricity to flow.

Water drops moving down a wire will rake off enough electrons to flash a small neon bulb which requires over 68 volts. This is comparable to sliding across a plastic seat and then experiencing an electric shock when you touch someone.

Water moving underground seems to cause or be associated with electric flow. Any time electricity flows in any kind of conductor, it creates an electromagnetic field, which can then be picked up by our internal sensors. Like the eye that can differentiate between forms, shades, and colors, the

Water Movement Generating Electricity

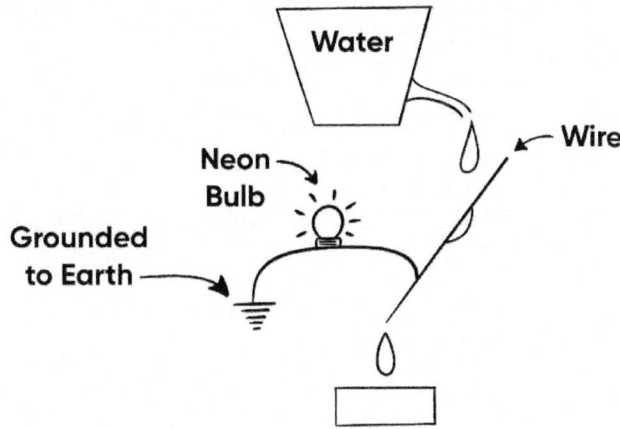

magnetic sensors, at least according to dowsing, seem to differentiate between patterns of electromagnetic energy fields from different sources. Likewise, the Subconscious can easily have information about the location of moving underground water.

Sharing Information from the Subconscious with the Conscious Mind

How does this information from the Subconscious get to the Conscious mind? Here is one way it may work. You may have heard of muscle testing, a procedure in which the Subconscious can be programmed to cause involuntary muscle movements to be strong for a true statement and weak for a false statement. It is used by many chiropractors, psychologists, complementary medical workers, etc. If you have not had this experience, find someone who knows how to do it and be amazed at how well it works! You can program the Subconscious to respond to any number of requests, including dowsing. Electronic muscle testing instruments attached to dowsers in action have shown what appear to be subconsciously controlled involuntary muscle movements which seem to affect the dowsing tool. There are probably many other factors involved, but this makes sense, and is a comfortable starting place for the mind.

Exploring How Map Dowsing is Powered: The Backster Effect

What I have described above makes sense for on-site dowsing, or being close to the water, but what about the map dowsing that most modern dowsers do? In map dowsing, a dowser can very often accurately and verifiably locate water and other things at great distance using only a dowsing device and a map or drawing. (Map dowsing is discussed in more detail later in this book.)

Map dowsing seems to be related to what is sometimes called the **Backster Effect.**[8] Backster was a lie detector specialist who attached a galvanic skin response device, which measures the electrical resistance of the skin to the top leaf of a plant. He then watered the plant, expecting to measure how long it

---

[8] Tompkins and Bird, <u>Secret Life of Plants,</u> Avon, 1974. Very informative book covering many aspects of the Backster Effect and much more.

would take for the water to reach the leaf and change its resistance. Instead, the lie detector immediately indicated what would be considered a "happy effect" in humans. Puzzled, he decided to see if could traumatize the plant by burning a leaf. The plant showed a fear response on the lie detector machine as soon as he had this thought. Backster's experiments have been duplicated thousands of times by many persons using many variations and have been well publicized on TV and in many books.

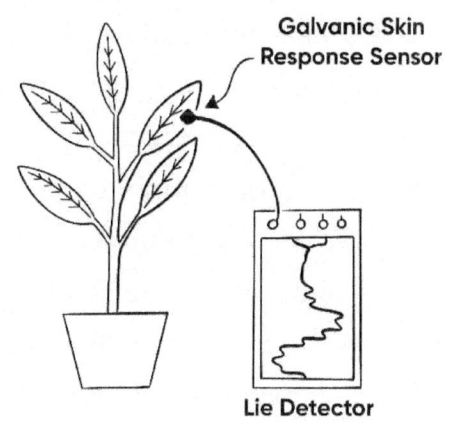

The Backster Effect

Galvanic Skin Response Sensor

Lie Detector

Experiments have shown that some type of energy that we might call "Superconscious" for lack of a better word, seems to have been flowing between Backster's mind and the plant. It turns out that this "Superconscious" seems to flow between and within all persons, animals, plants, and most everything, including our Subconscious which somehow taps into this information. Have you ever felt ill-at-ease or apprehensive for no apparent reason? Or have you ever wondered how a mother somehow knows if something bad is happening to her child when the child and mother may be many miles apart? The Superconciousness may be the explanation for these phenomena as well.

If your Subconscious has access to this "Superconscious" and you have access to the Subconscious with your dowsing device, it seems that you can tap into a lot of information. Why might your conscious mind not have constant access to the Subconscious? The apparent reason is the danger of an overload. Just think what billions of bits of continuously in-flowing information from your Subconscious would do to your concentration. The dowsing instrument allows you to tap the Subconscious selectively when you need to obtain useful information. While there is much more to understanding how dowsing works than I have described, we have made a good start.[9] [10] [11] Have fun exploring new ideas!

What Tools Do Dowsers Use?

A dowsing tool appears to be simply a read-out, interface, or communication device. It seems to be controlled through or by our Subconscious, or something of that nature, although I'm sure there are many other factors involved.

---

[9] " Electronic Pollution," Popular Science, Dec. 1983.

[10] " More Experiments in Electroculture" Popular Electronics, June 1971. Simple device that can be easily and simply made, with directions for its use. *(Low level electronic assembly skills required.)* There is also an overall discussion of the Backster Effect.

[11] Stone, The Secret Life of Your Cells. Whitford Press, 1989. Explores the research of Cleve Backster.

There are many very successful dowsing systems and methods, with or without tools, but as a general rule, most dowsers usually use some type of dowsing tool. We will cover the four most popular types which are the **Pendulum, L Rods, Y Rod, and Bobber.** You will also find unlimited variations in shape, size, materials that they are made of, and how they are used. This variety does not seem to affect their workability other than speed, agility or convenience. Many dowsers have a whole pile of dowsing tools that they have collected or made. These tools generally fit into one or some combination of the above. Choice of tool may depend on which one is handy or quickly made, e.g., by cutting a clothes hanger or hanging some object on a string. Usually, it is just the most convenient one for a particular job. Dowsing devices come in all sizes, shapes, and materials. It doesn't seem to matter very much to most experienced dowsers what the dowsing tool is made of. Although many dowsers have their favorites, and some even swear by a particular tool that works well for them, it appears that all the dowsing tools seem to work equally well when used by experienced dowsers. It is what you get used to, and what feels good to you, that should determine your choice.

The following is a short description of the four basic instruments commonly used for dowsing.

Pendulum

Pendulum

Shape: Can be anything that you can hang on a string or chain. It can be any size, even as small as a paper-clip on a thread. The chain or string is usually about three to four inches long.

Materials: Anything you can find.

How to Use: Hold as shown. The usual response request is swinging straight forward for YES, sideways for NO, and at an angle for "Ready for Question". Feel free to instruct (*direct, Program*) your dowsing system to respond in any way you would like.

Advantages: Easy to make. Easy to use. Very popular. Small enough to go in your pocket or purse. Quick response. Excellent tool for dowsing charts or maps.

Disadvantages: Pendulums can be problematic in windy conditions or when walking. This problem can be overcome by requesting (*pre-arranging, Programming*) the pendulum to spin in a clockwise or counterclockwise direction to indicate the YES or NO response.

L Rods (Angle Rod, Swing Rod, Pointing Rod, etc.)

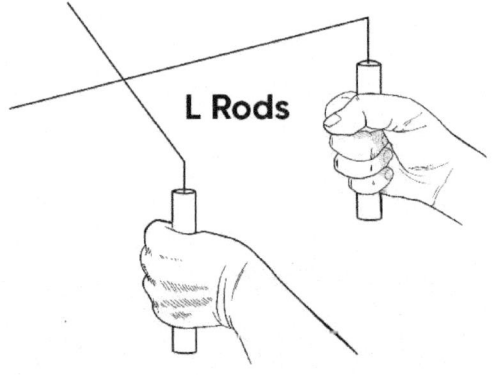

Material: Usually wire. Metal coat hangers work well. Welding rods are also a very popular. You can use just about anything you can bend into the L shape.

How to Use: Hold loosely in your hand with the top wire tilted slightly downward.

When one L Rod is used alone, it acts as a pointer or a swing rod. It can be requested to point towards a target or direction, or to swing sideways when meeting a specified energy field, such as an aura or noxious zone. These will be discussed later in the book.

When using two L Rods program them normally to point straight forward for the ready position, to cross for the YES response or when over a target, and to swing outward for the NO response.

Advantages: Easy to make. Easy to use. Very versatile and popular. Work well when walking over rough ground. They are generally not affected by mild winds.

Disadvantages: Not as easy to carry or conceal as a pendulum, although the small 4 - 6 inch ones can be put in your shirt pocket or purse.

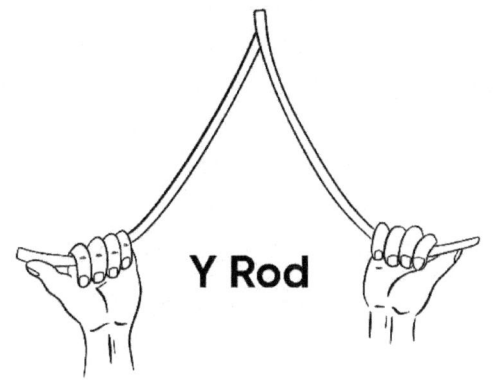

Y Rod (Forked Stick, Talking Stick, etc.)

Shape: Traditionally, it is a forked stick that looks like the letter Y. It can be any size, usually around 12 to 24 inches in length.

Material: Can be wood, metal, or plastic. Plastic ones are popular with many dowsers, probably because of its ease of storage.

How to Use: Hold with pointed end down. Your thumbs will be up and palms will be facing each other. Hold tight and spread Y Rod outward while rotating your wrist outward. Your thumbs will now be pointed outward, and your palms will be up. The Y Rod will flip up into a delicate balance.

Pointing upward at an angle of around 45° is usually used for the "Ready", or "Ready for Question" position.

The Y Rod will swing down from the "Ready" position to point at a water vein or target. This may also be used for the YES response.

Swinging up from the ready position is usually used for the NO response.

Advantages: Acts quickly, can point directly towards a water vein or target. Works well while walking over rough ground. Reliable in fairly strong winds.

Disadvantages: Not as versatile as other dowsing tools. It only has an up and down motion. You will need to turn your body to find direction.

Bobber (Wand, Spring Rod, Divining Rod, etc.)

Shape: Any flexible rod, branch or wire. Can be almost any length from one foot to over three feet. It sometimes has a coiled wire and a weighted tip.

Material: Anything that is flexible, but apply some protection for a sharp end to avoid accidental scratches.

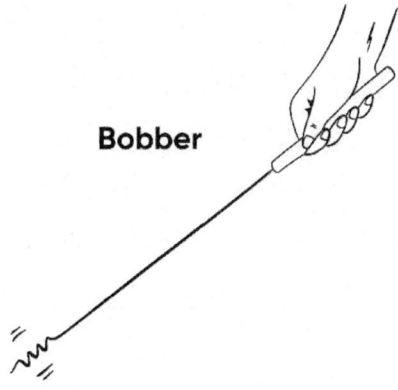

Bobber

How to Use: Hold it down at around 45°. You can program it to simply mimic a pendulum by bobbing up and down for YES, sideways for NO, and 45° for "Ready for Question". Or you may simply request what you want different bobber responses to represent. For example, swinging side to side when pointing in the direction of a requested target, and to spinning when over the target.

Advantages: Can replace a pendulum for field work. Most dowsers find it easy to use. Larger sizes are often easier to see in demonstrations with people standing in a circle.

Disadvantages: Won't usually fit in your pocket or purse.

What Are Dowsing Charts?

Charts come in every conceivable form that you can imagine. There are books of dowsing charts. To start, look at the *"YES/NO Chart"* below. This is all you will need most of the time for YES and NO questions. You can use the "Ready for Question" line or simply start your pendulum swinging in an area away from any answer. This way you know it is not stuck over an answer.

If you don't have a printed chart handy when you want to dowse, you can use your hand, held out horizontally, letting your thumb or index finger make a right angle. These will work for YES and NO, while a swing diagonally between them can be the Ready for Question signal.

YES / NO Chart

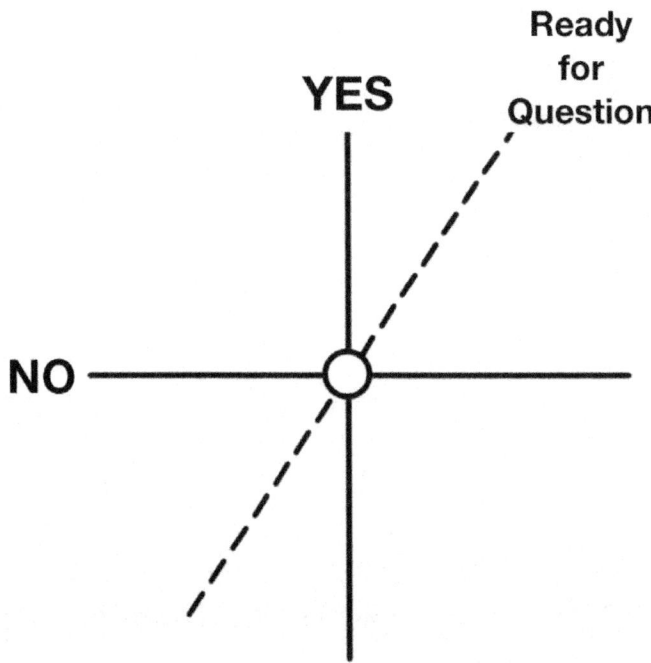

Detailed Instructions for Pendulum Dowsing

We will start with the pendulum. If you are in a class, your instructor will probably have several types of dowsing tools to play with. But for now, we will use a commonly used tool - the pendulum. It is normally used with a dowsing chart. Your instructor might choose L Rods first, as they are just as easy to learn to use as a pendulum.

Pendulum

Holding the Pendulum

Generally, you hold the pendulum like in the picture above. The length of the string or chain between your finger and the pendulum determines how fast it moves. A string or chain held around 3-4 inches above the weight will usually give a good swing speed. Because this is a subconscious training or programming procedure, like training your subconscious bioelectrical muscle system to use any device, it is not critical how you hold the dowsing tool as long as it is comfortable and functional. When you write your name with a pen, which you already have a Program for, you start the pen and expect it (focused intent) to automatically write your name, and it does. You will be training your Subconscious to independently, without your help, move the pendulum in response to your questions.

31

Don't let anyone tell you that your fingers are not supposed to move. In the lab, if you take fast-frame motion pictures, you can see these non-deliberate, Subconsciously controlled movements on any dowser. The motion is sometimes subtle and small, but it is there.

Using Your Pendulum

To begin, hang your pendulum directly over the center of the cross, or the bottom of the half circle of *"YES/NO Chart"* above, and deliberately start the pendulum swinging toward "Ready for Question". Physically make it go.[12] This is to start training your Subconscious bioelectrical muscle system. It will probably stop. Start it again. You are starting to create a working Program. Now, while you have it swinging to "Ready for Question", make it work its way to the YES and then back to "Ready for Question". Now do the same thing for NO. Each time, you will be deliberately helping to keep the pendulum swinging. Practice these maneuvers several times. In just a few minutes, it will

---

[12] While, you can control the movement of dowsing tools, or your pen when writing, you can also let the Subconscious control the movement. This is like writing your signature. One way to do this is to treat the pendulum or other tool like a person. When you ask a person a serious question, you simply watch and listen for an answer. If you think about what you are doing, you will notice that you go into a kind of silence. You are just watching and listening, without thinking or even being aware of anything else except the response. When you dowse, try going into this "silence" and just watch and wait for the answer. This is sometimes called the "Dowsing Mode". Once you start the pendulum swinging, ask questions, and let the Subconscious take over. You will be amazed how well it works! Dowsing does take practice but can be learned rather quickly.

be working just a little on its own. It will be then time to move to the *"Learning to Dowse"* section.

The pendulum's movement from the center towards "Ready for Question" is the Indicating Half Swing. Ignore the back swing from the center away from "Ready for Question", pretend you can't see it. Follow only the "Indicating Forward Swing" wherever it goes - even if it goes down to the bottom half on some types of circle charts.

Walt Woods

Learning to Dowse

Learning to dowse is like learning to play a musical instrument or learning to type. It requires carefully controlled instructions and practice. As with a musical instrument, the rewards can be very pleasant and useful.

What Are Some Good Dowsing Habits

Try these *"Ten Steps to Successful Dowsing."* Just follow the instructions systematically, doing one step at a time. Each step is very easy and doesn't take very long to do.

Did you know?

Experienced dowsers seem to be able to share some of their dowsing energies with those dowsing around them. New dowsers may benefit from practicing with an experienced dowser for many reasons!

Time and Place

Try to find a quiet place where you can be alone and where you feel comfortable, and a spot that would normally be available to you at the same time each day for a few minutes of practice. This is like making an appointment with your Subconscious or Spirit Guides. This place might be the kitchen table early in the morning, or sitting up in bed late at night, or any other time or place. If you are with other dowsers or you have already developed some skill, it won't be as important to be in your special place at a predetermined time.

Getting Started - The First Six Steps

To begin, read the following six steps all the way through, so you will have an idea of what you will be doing. You don't need to study them, just become familiar with them. Then come back and go through them one step at a time.

Step 1. Relax. Become quiet and drift into a prayerful mode. This is the brain's alpha state[13].

Step 2. Take your pendulum *(any pendulum will do)* and hold the string or chain between your thumb and first finger. Hold it with about 1½ to 3 inches of string length between the pendulum itself and your fingertips. Next, hold the pendulum over the center of the *"YES/NO Chart"* on the following page.

---

[13] Alpha State in the brain is described as a state of wakeful relaxation that is associated with increased alpha wave activity. When electroencephalograms show a brain wave pattern of 9 to 12 cycles per second, the subject is said to be in *alpha state,* usually described as relaxed, peaceful, or floating.

YES / NO Chart

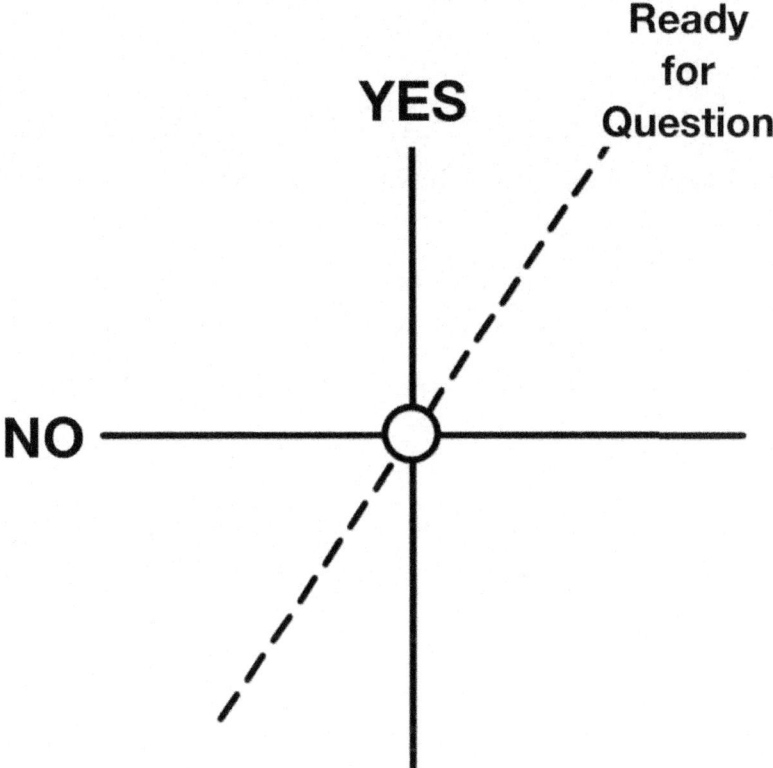

Step 3. Now, manually *(by moving your hand and fingers)* make the pendulum start swinging towards the YES. Ask, and expect it to keep swinging on its own without your help. Ask it out loud with about the same normal speaking voice and tone as talking to a person. If it stops, start it over again, and ask it to keep going. Watch only the upper or forward half of the pendulum's swing and

ignore the other half, from the center towards you. Repeat until the pendulum keeps swinging on its own. You will be deliberately starting the pendulum and then asking it to keep swinging with no added help from you. You are simply training your system to react in a predetermined way.

Step 4. Do the same thing for the NO. Your fingers are still over the center of the circle, and you are ignoring one half of the swing.

Step 5. Once it is swinging by itself to NO, ask it, while it is still swinging, to work its way clockwise back to YES and then continue to "Ready for Question".

Step 6. Next, ask it to work its way counter-clockwise from "Ready for Question" to YES and to NO, and then clockwise back to YES. Practice Steps 3, 4, 5 and 6 several times.

Practicing with a Pendulum and Chart

When you are comfortable using of the first six steps, you can begin practicing using a pendulum and a chart to receive answers to questions. Using the *"YES/NO Chart"*, and with your pendulum swinging toward "Ready for Question", ask several questions whose answers you already know. This gives you an opportunity to visually, mentally, emotionally, and subconsciously experience the sensation of your pendulum swinging to the right answer. It is okay to encourage the pendulum. Even if you think you are influencing the answer, <u>it is still the correct answer</u>. You will be working with your Subconscious. Here are some suggested questions you could try.

➤ Is my name Joe? (YES or NO)

➤ Am I female? (YES or NO)

➤ Do I live in Chico? (YES or NO)

This sounds too simple, but do not underestimate the pleasant feelings of control you just gave your Subconscious. For fun, you might try some unknown areas. If you sometimes get the wrong answer, don't fret. Even the most experienced dowsers occasionally miss the mark. (The reason for this and some suggested remedies will be explained later.) Treat dowsing as an interesting and exciting learning adventure. Enjoy!

L-Rod Practice

If you are in a class, ask your instructor to find and mark a water vein or energy zone. Now with your L Rod(s) in the Ready position (pointing straight ahead) go to the spot they marked and expect your rods to react the same way the instructor's rods reacted. Your positive attitude prepares you to experience visual, mental, emotional, and subconscious success. If you don't have an instructor, find a water valve and experience finding a known pipe. Once you have this positive dowsing reaction, go play and have fun! Getting your L-Rod(s) into the Ready position invites your Subconscious to participate.

If you were not able to accomplish the above in about 15 minutes, try again in about half an hour or the next day. Don't give up, try again. Success will come as you do so.

Before continuing to the next steps, you will need to have some understanding about Programming your dowsing system and its purpose.

Preparing to Program Your Dowsing System

Sometimes it can be very helpful to have an experienced dowser help you when you are just starting out.[14] On the other hand, this procedure can usually be done all by yourself by simply using the following directions.

---

[14] Going to a dowsing club meeting is an excellent way to get acquainted with other dowsers and find both help and encouragement. Contact the American Society of Dowsers at dowsers.org for locations of meetings and other information.

Letter to Robin

Programming Your Dowsing System

Programming, or informing your Subconscious of what you want, is very simple. Any time you learn something new, you have created a new, additional, or add-on Program. For example, you can inform your Subconscious to alert you to pick up a loaf of bread the next time you are in a grocery store. It can do this. On a more permanent basis, you can program it to turn out the light each time you leave a certain room. Some people can even program their Subconscious to wake them at 6 o'clock every morning, and it will. In the above cases, you needed to inform your Subconscious in advance. It does not automatically know what you want it to do. It's easy to program it with the details of what you want to know, and how it is to indicate the answers to your questions.

Definition of a Program

At the time of this writing, Webster's Dictionary[15] states that "a program is a plan or system under which action may be taken towards a goal". Establishing agreed upon conditions with your Dowsing System is a form of Programming.

---

[15] Merriam-Webster's Collegiate Dictionary (10th ed.). (1999). Merriam-Webster Incorporated.

Purpose of Programming

The purpose of Programming is to achieve maximum accuracy. This is done by establishing some mutually acceptable, pre-established, agreements and understandings about words, phrases, conditions, and what is meant by different pendulum or dowsing tool movements with your Dowsing System.

If you have succeeded in getting your pendulum to move to "YES" and "NO", and back and forth between them, and have practiced a little bit, you are ready to proceed with Programming your Dowsing System. Read through these steps first to get the overall idea.

Three Steps to Programming Your Dowsing System

Once you have your pendulum or L Rod trained or Programmed to move to YES and NO, it is time to inform your Dowsing System what you are interested in. It needs to know what parameters to use and how to respond to your questions.

Program Installation is very easy, there are just three simple steps.

Letter to Robin

1. Obtain Permission

Use the *"YES/NO Chart"* for this exercise. With your pendulum swinging to "Ready for Question", ask the Dowsing System the following question (*It is best to read the question out loud*):

"May I, Can I, Should I, establish, change, or add Dowsing Conditions and Agreements or Programs which will be continually in effect until changed by me?"

➤ If the pendulum swings to YES, go to step 2.

➤ If the pendulum goes to NO, then try again at a later time.

2. Input or Establish a Program

If your pendulum swings to YES, then read (*preferably out loud*) a prepared Program. In Step 7-1, you will learn how to program your first Program. Your pendulum should continue to keep swinging to YES while you read any Program, change, or addition to a Program. Finish by saying, *"End of prearranged conditions and agreements. Thank you,"* or just simply say, *"End of Program. Thank you."* There are some suggested Programs in the *"Programs"* section, of which this text will go into depth with, as well as explaining adding items or making changes to Programs a little later in this text.

Holding the pendulum at the edge of your side vision, in your peripheral view, as you read your Program will have a post-hypnotic effect. This helps to semi-permanently store the Program in your Subconscious, until you wish to make deletions, adjustments, or additions.

3. **Final Check**

Ask the Dowsing System:

"Are the Conditions or Changes acceptable as presented, being clear and non-contradictory, and open to change by my request?"

➤ If YES, you are finished.

➤ If NO, use your pendulum to ask questions and try to determine why. Repeat the installation process with improved wording.

You are programming your Subconscious or Dowsing System, not the pendulum or L Rod, and you do not have to repeat Programs each time you dowse. Your Subconscious will automatically respond to your pre-programmed instructions, just as when you are driving your car or playing a musical instrument.

Once you input Programs into the Dowsing System you do not have to repeat the programming process each time you want to use them. They are automatically and continually in effect until changed by you.

Program Installation

The following _Foundation or Primary Programs_ were developed over several years with the input of many dowsers. If you have an instructor, they will probably have changes, additions, or improvements based on their experiences.

> **You don't have to understand the reasons for the programming instructions. Your Subconscious is very well-informed and will easily understand and use these instructions. New instructions may be added to overcome problems that become apparent to practicing dowsers. You will probably add more instructions in the future.**

To install a Program, use the three-step system:

1. Get permission.

2. Read a prepared Program with the pendulum running in the YES mode.

3. Ask your Dowsing System if the Program is okay. If YES, you are done. If NO, you may dialog with your System by asking questions and using YES and NO responses to find out why. Make appropriate changes to the Program and read the new version as in step 2.

Step 7-1. Primary (or Foundation) Program Introduction and Installation

The *"Primary Program"* is your foundation Program on which all subsequent programs are based. Install it first. You will be surprised how easy it is!

If you have established permission (Step 1) and gotten a YES, then with your pendulum swinging to "YES", read out loud the following suggested *"Primary Program"*. In the future, you may wish to make changes to this and other Programs. This Program is listed in its entirety, as are all the other Programs in this book, in the *"Programs"* section (pages 67 to 69).

Primary Program: is to be continually in effect until I choose to make changes.

- *It covers the overall primary controls, limits, agreements, and dowsing responses.*

Letter to Robin

- **The Purpose** *is to determine amounts, effects, conditions, circumstances, influences, times, measurements, distances, numbers, percentages, and other requested areas.*

- **Communications and Support** *are to be inter-cooperative and restricted to my Superconscious, Spirit, Higher Self, My Awareness, Mind Systems, Subconscious and related systems, and all other levels of my Total Being and their approved Spirit Guides/Guardian Angels, helpers, and others chosen by me, or any of the above.*

- **Influences** *such as misleading thoughts, imaging, wishes, or any other conditions or methods by any source, physical or non-physical, of any kind, are not to take control of any of my systems or affect me adversely or cause incorrect dowsing answers.*

- **Time,** *as related to dowsing, is to be in my perceived time unless otherwise requested.*

- **Answers** *are to be selected from all available knowledge and information sources.*

- **The Method of Answering** *by the pendulum or any dowsing systems is to be:*

    (a) *Swinging to (?) -or- "Ready for Question" or other agreed upon methods or systems, indicates "Ready for Question".*

    (b) *General swinging, or moving to "YES", "NO", or other information indicating the most appropriate answer for the question asked, or other information methods or systems.*

    (c) *Clockwise spinning is for hold, indicating waiting, searching, or other agreed upon systems.*

- **Temporary Changes** *to any dowsing Program may be made by me while dowsing, automatically reverting to the original Program after use.*

- **Program Changes,** *like adding, deleting, or changing, may be made by me, but only by using a three-step system[16] of my choice.*

- **End of Program.** *Thank you.*

---

[16] The three-step requirement in a Program, like the three steps you use to install this Program, is to prevent accidental changes without your deliberate intent. Review the steps in detail on pages 44-46.

Letter to Robin

Step 7-2. Request for Guidance Program Introduction and Installation

If we are dealing with our Subconscious, Superconscious, Spirit Guides, and probably many other aspects of our being, we need their guidance and support. If you ask for guidance and get a "YES", then all these aspects will help you achieve your goal. If you get a "NO" from your guidance request, don't be surprised if you are blocked or get no support, or get wrong answers. There are many reasons not to proceed. For example, if your Spirit Guides have spent a year setting you up, or someone else, to learn a very valuable life lesson, and you wish to change or interfere with it, you would probably get a "NO". It is okay to dialogue with your Dowsing System and ask why.

The following is the Program I currently use to request guidance. It is also known as the *"May I, Can I, Should I...? Program"*. There are many versions of these principles, and I will probably change these as I learn more.

The three-step installation time is about 45 seconds.

(1) Get permission.

(2) Read the Program

(3) Check to see if it's okay.

__May I, Can I, Should I...? Program:__ is to become a working part of all my Dowsing Programs and be continually in effect until I choose to make changes. When used in reference to dowse questions, the "May I, Can I, Should I" is to have the following meaning:

May I is to mean: *Do I have appropriate permission to proceed and be involved?*

Can I is to mean: *Do I have the ability to successfully dowse in this area, and am I ready?*

Should I is to mean: *Considering all aspects related to this situation, would it be appropriate, proper, and suitable to dowse in this area?*

End of Program. *Thank you.*

Final Check

Step 8. Go back to the three-step installation Program and check to see if it is okay. If the answer is YES, you have properly installed these Programs. Other Program installations are just as easy. If NO is indicated, ask inquiring questions as to why, make any corrections needed, and repeat steps 2 and 3.

About Your Programming

Once you have programmed your Dowsing System, you will have instructions and agreements that are as thorough, detailed, and as carefully thought out as an experienced dowser's. The nice part is that you don't have to remember all the details of the Programs. Your Subconscious will do it for you. The programmed information is in your Subconscious and will be automatically in effect when you dowse. It's like using your mind to move your finger. The Subconscious has a program to move your finger already. All you must do is desire, with your mind, for your finger to move, and it does. The Subconscious, based on your desire, activates the appropriate program for your finger to move. With your dowsing device, you asked the dowsing system if it would install Programs relating to your dowsing, and it has.

You are now ready for the last but **extremely important** Steps 9 and 10.

> **You don't have to know how your finger or dowsing Programs work.**
>
> **Just use them.**

Step 9. Preferably in your favorite spot, your favorite appointment time, and with your pendulum working well, you will need to ask some practice questions to which you have no emotional attachment. An example question might be, "What is the effect of my vitamin C level?" You don't emotionally care if it's a little high or a little low. It is not like a question about your lost kitten about which you may be feeling very anxious and upset. Use the *Personal Dowsing Chart* on the next page (also in the *Charts* section of this book) Try asking for "Level of Effects" on how it seems to affect your system. Use the Normal, Mild, Strong, and Very Strong sections.

Personal Dowsing Chart

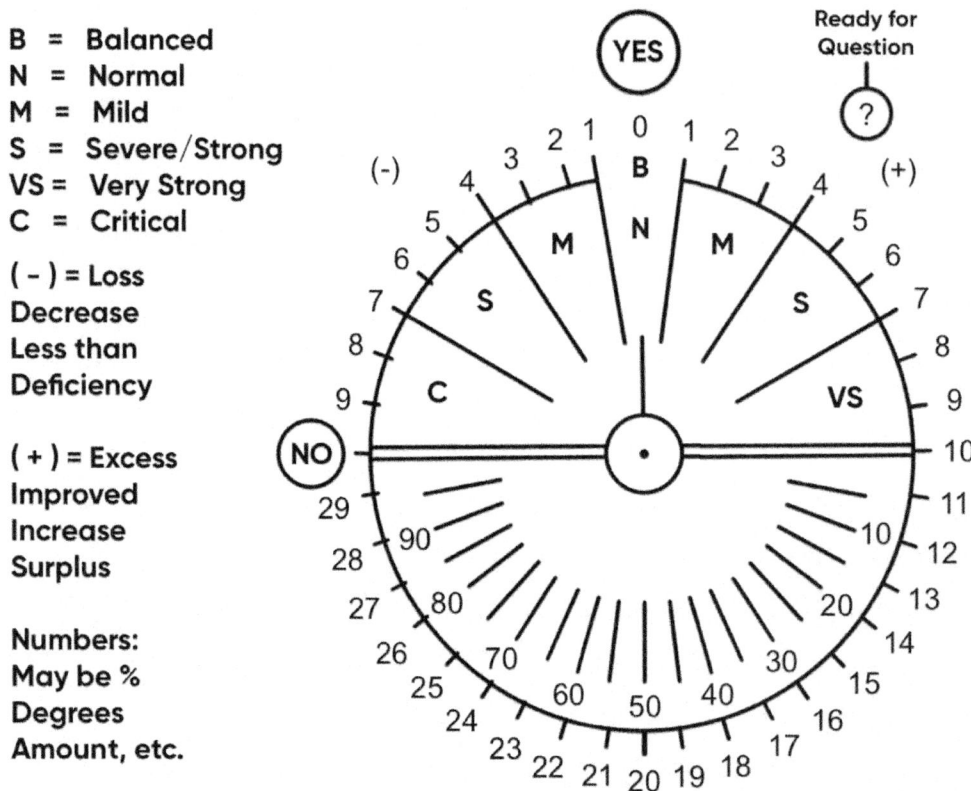

B = Balanced
N = Normal
M = Mild
S = Severe/Strong
VS = Very Strong
C = Critical

(-) = Loss
Decrease
Less than
Deficiency

(+) = Excess
Improved
Increase
Surplus

Numbers:
May be %
Degrees
Amount, etc.

If, for example, (to your vitamin C question) it indicates a minus 3 (*-M or mildly non-beneficial*). Then you might ask what the effect would be if you took 500 milligrams of vitamin C. It would probably go to +3 or +4 (*+M or mildly beneficial*). There are many topics that you might play with. Pick those that you are not emotionally concerned with, or for which you have prior definite knowledge of the answer. The Dowsing System will automatically answer your question using your previously installed Programs.[17]

Changing the Basic Dowsing Subject

It is very important that each time you change the basic dowsing subject, you should ask the Dowsing System "May I, Can I, Should I...?" If the answer is YES, proceed. If NO, trust its judgement. Guidance is what you are wisely seeking. It is permissible to ask why.

When Can You Trust Your Dowsing?

Every day, as suggested in Step 9, play with a few questions for 5 to 10 minutes and then end your session with a final check. There are some fun questions to practice with in the accompanying practice journal, *The Fruitful Search: Letter to Robin Dowsing Practice Companion Journal.* To do this, ask your pendulum to work its way clockwise to the lower side of the circle using the ***Personal Dowsing Chart***. Here you will find a number scale that will go from 0 to 100. Ask the pendulum what percent influence your personal feelings or free will had on the answers. (*Watch only the indicating part of the pendulum swing. You are now using the lower half of the circle. The pendulum is now indicating toward the*

---

[17] See also **Over 100 Possible Questions** and the **Caution** on page 95.

bottom.) Even though you asked the Subconscious, in your **Primary Program** not to allow you to interfere, there is a deeper stronger Program that prevents the Subconscious from interfering with your free will. If you are strong-minded, or over-anxious, you can override your dowsing Programming. Don't be surprised if your pendulum indicates that you are influencing your answers as much as 20% to 30% when you are a beginner. Each day when you do the above practice, *deliberately trying* not to influence the answers, the percent will become less and less. After a while the percent will go to 0 most of the time and you will achieve a breakthrough where you very rarely influence the answers. At this point you may trust your dowsing to a much greater extent.

Step 10. When you feel more secure and trusting of your Dowsing System, ask the pendulum if you should re-enter the **Primary Program.** If the answer is YES, do it. If NO, then you are properly programmed and may enter other Programs, invent new ones, or make changes. You are now free to advance as you wish. The sky is the limit!

Practicing Dowsing

Have fun and practice for a few minutes each day. It's like playing a musical instrument - if you carefully follow the instructions and practice a little bit each day, your skill and accuracy will improve. Don't become discouraged if you are not right all the time. Even the best dowsers sometimes have interference or a bad day.[18]

Different Instruments

It is good to develop your skills using your favorite dowsing tool for questions about areas of special interest to you. You will then find it much easier learning to use the other dowsing tools. Most people with good dowsing skills have their favorites, but can usually use the Pendulum, Y Rod, L Rod, and Bobber or some variation.

---

[18] Editor's note: Interferences can come from a variety of sources that can negatively influence and alter the accuracy of your dowsing. These can include but are not limited to noxious energies, strong emotions (both positive and negative), negative nonphysical entities, energy vortexes (both positive and negative), etc. When dowsing in a new location or with a new client, it is important that you set your intention to limit or block all interferences while you work.

Formulating Useful Dowsing Questions

The Three Rules

An often-repeated story among experienced dowsers illustrates the importance of wording dowsing questions carefully. One time, a veteran dowser/instructor asked his L Rod to point to "north" during a presentation. Instead of pointing to "magnetic north", it pointed to the audience. Surprised, he asked again with the same result. While he was discussing some possible causes with the audience, a hand went up and a man said, "My name is North." The dowsing was 100% correct for the question asked. I suspect the dowser then changed the question, asking for the rod to point to earth's magnetic north, and then got a correct answer. This proves a very important point about being precise in your question.

Another example might be the question, "Does my car need gas?" The answer would be YES, even if the gas tank is full. The answer is YES on two accounts. First, you have a gasoline car which can only run on what we call "gas", and secondly, it uses air which is also a gas. So, of course it needs gas! The Dowsing System seems to take every word in a question by its literal meaning. If your question has a word or words that have assumed or conflicting meanings, your answer may be unexpected, confusing, or even incorrect.

Rule #1: Be Specific. What do you want to know? This includes what, where, when, and sometimes instructional information relating to the question.

Rule #2: Use only words, phrases, and conditions for which you and the Dowsing System have an agreed upon meaning, and for which there is an agreed upon method of dowsing response. For example, YES, NO, or Not available at this time.

Rule #3: Make the question a definite request for information that exists somewhere. Avoid asking for an opinion. If your question involves an opinion of the past, present, or the future, it must be compared to an agreed upon reference or condition. For example, if I asked you, "Are you strong?" your answer would be based on what you think I meant by the word "strong"? Did I mean strong physically? mentally? emotionally? Did you have on strong perfume? etc. Now let us apply rules 1, 2, and 3. I'll ask the question again, "Are you strong enough, right now, to pick up this one-gallon carton of milk?" Could you give me a correct answer to that question now?

If I ask, "How many feet are there from point (A) to point (B) on the floor, by the front row of the audience?" the answer might be twelve because there are six persons sitting in that space, each with two feet. My meaning of the word, "feet", may not have been the same as that of the Dowsing System.

Some Tips for Developing Good Dowsing Questions

• **Formulating the Question:** When you wish to explore a new area where you have not already established questions, ask several similar questions, looking for agreement or conflicting answers. Conflicts may help you uncover additional unrecognized factors that could help you ask a more precise question.

> *Q. Is there water in the [designate the area]?*
>
> *A. The answer is YES. (There is water everywhere, in the grass etc.)*

> *Q. Is there a water source, less than 300 feet deep, that could supply 5 GPM (gallons-per-minute)?*
>
> *A. The answer is YES. (Especially in a hard rainstorm).*

The next question may give you a clue that something is wrong.

> *Q. Could this water source, allow a well to supply 5 GPM of potable water to the surface, year around?*
>
> *A. If the answer is NO, you then know something was wrong with the first questions.*

By asking multiple questions you can often find problems and learn to develop better, more comprehensive questions.

- **Take time to focus your mind on the question you wish to ask.** If you have tried to clear your mind in preparation for meditation, you have probably experienced your thoughts darting everywhere. Don't assume the Subconscious can tell exactly what you want from the jumble of changing thoughts. Not until you deliberately focus and carefully word a question can the Subconscious Dowsing System know exactly what you want to ask.

- **Pre-Programming:** With your Programming you have prevented a great many of the possible misunderstandings that may occur between you and your Dowsing System. This is one of the important reasons that you have established Programs, or agreements, with your Dowsing System.

- **Comparing Results with Another Experienced Dowser:** Another way that seems to work well, especially when you have a very important question, is to get together with another experienced dowser. If you each ask the question in your own way and have the same answer, it is reassuring. If you get different answers, you should both examine your questions and then repeat the process.

• **Be Careful of Questions Involving the Future:** In my experience, at this level, our Subconscious, Higher Self, Superconscious, Spirit Guides, etc., seem to have wonderful abilities and almost unlimited information sources. It appears they are very rarely wrong, but the answers are based on the literal interpretation of our questions. Predicting seems to work at times, but it could be based on their vast knowledge of ongoing and/or past events.

Prediction Question Example

"If I left for work every Monday at 8 o'clock for the last three years, could I predict what I will be doing in a week or a month from now, on Monday at 8 o'clock, with pretty good accuracy?"

**Please fill in your name,
address, and sign here.**

**Let's see: Mary Jones
1012 High St., Capricorn**

Age of parents if "living"?

Mom 105, Dad 106

**Are they really that old?
No, but they would be if still living.**

The clients' answers in the above cartoons were based on different meanings of "sign" and "if living" than were intended by the questioner.

The Question Test

It is a good idea to use questions that have worked well before and test new ones. Test them, as suggested in *"Formulating the Question"*, above, by asking the question several different ways to see if you repeatedly get an appropriate answer each time. This procedure makes you think carefully about what the words mean and if you have left anything out of the question or Program.

We use many popular expressions in our everyday communications like: "He will get a kick out of this", "Hang your head in shame", "She has a chip on her shoulder", "Time will tell", etc. that do not mean literally what they say. Using them in dowsing questions could result in an incorrect or misleading response. I often ask a question in two different ways, which is an approach that helps me catch problem wording.

A Personal Preparation Checklist for Choosing Good Dowsing Questions

Always check personal dowsing readiness first with the following nine questions as a single block.

Letter to Robin

1: Pre-Check:

- Please indicate the lowest level of effectiveness for: (1) my readiness (2) interference blocking (3) obtaining information (4) abilities (5) response ability (6) relating (7) interpretation.

2: Permission:

- May I, Can I, Should I dowse [myself]?

- If the answer is "NO" it's okay to ask why.

3-8 Most Detrimental, Non-beneficial, Interfering and Undesirable Effects, Impacts, Influences for:

3: Entities? Outside Influences?

- (From people, noxious energies, psychic, etc. - within the last [24 hours] or as requested.)

4: Thought Forms?

- (Images, Imprints, Ideas, Experiences, Race Consciousness, etc. These include present and past lives.)

5: Conditions? Other Influences?

- (Within the last [24 hours] **See "100+ Areas" on page 95.**

6: Mind - Body - Spirit Connections or Alignment?

- (For all aspects of [my] total being - Mind, etc.)

7: Ability to receive and send beneficial influences?

- (For any reading less than desired see Q5-8 below.)

8: Personal Concerns or Conditions?

- (Areas of special personal interest needing extra attention.)

9: Safety Net:

- Please indicate the lowest level of effectiveness for: (1) Connections, (2) Information, (3) Abilities, (4) Time/Space, (5) Interference, (6) Omissions, (7) Results (Normally requested as a single block.)

10 Completeness of requested changes as 0-100%:

- (After you indicate for your "now", clock or calendar times.)

Possible Responses to A Personal Preparation Checklist for Choosing Good Dowsing Questions

1: Your Readiness.

The first question is designed to do just this. It does this by looking for the lowest level of effectiveness for seven different broad-spectrum areas. I usually ask for the lowest level of effectiveness for the entire block. If it is less than +/-1 on the cycle chart, I proceed to isolate the individual component. Once I find where the problem is, I can run corrections before proceeding. I personally don't like to work in any areas where I am knowingly or unknowingly blocked, inappropriately influenced, or not ready in some component of my "System".

2: Permission. If YES, proceed. If NO tactful avoidance is advisable. Trust the advice.

I don't like to interfere with someone else's life without first checking in and obtaining permission to proceed.

3: If *Entities*, ask "Medics" from the Entity's world to pick them up and give them appropriate medical care. If *Thought Forms* from the outside, ask The System to adjust the aura to convert them to positive useful energies. This is a win/win situation.[19]

4: If a negative reading, try asking The System to first remove the emotional energies. Watch the pendulum for progress. (Working over to a +10) Then return pendulum to the original negative reading and ask the System to modify the thought forms, images, or imprints to neutral or beneficial, considering all aspect of [my] total being, including attitude. Watch the pendulum for progress.

5-8: For any undesirable readings, ask The System if it can and will adjust or modify these conditions. If "YES" ask The System to return the pendulum to

---

[19] Editor's note: Within several shamanic traditions, it is believed that within each world, dimension, or level of consciousness, there are both beneficial entities and nonbeneficial entities. We believe that what Walt is referring to in this instance is to call upon healer spirits from the entity's own realm to provide assistance so as to limit the amount of negative interference from wounded entities who we may have inadvertently called upon within our dowsing work.

the original reading and please proceed indicating progress with the pendulum. Recheck Question 4.

9: Possible Omissions

> This Program is intended to look for areas that I may have failed to think of or that I have not built into my overall Programming. It also instructs The System on the areas you want to be sure that it checks.

10: Required completeness time for requested changes.

> You may have asked for something to be done and The System agreed but gives you no clue as to when. It could be seconds, hours, days, or a lifetime before the changes are complete. The Subconscious of the person involved may rebel, must get used to the idea, or only partially accept the energies, etc. If you ask the percentage of completeness for different amounts of time, you will have a better idea what is going on. It may alert you to use a different approach. I normally start with a procedure by asking The System to check questions 1 and 2 through question 9 on myself as a block. If I get a +10, I'm ready to proceed. (This information on checking as a block would be useful at the beginning of the checking system and can save a lot of time. Only investigate if things are not +10.)

Question 1 Pre-Check Program

The Question 1 Pre-Check Program: *is to become part of and work with all of my Programs or agreements, and to be continually in effect until I choose to make changes. Considering all aspects of my selected "System" for communications, contact, corrections, and activities, please Indicate the Least Effective Level of Effectiveness for:*

(1)   My readiness, ability, and the response conditions necessary for information accuracy,

(2)   Interferences to obtaining information or achieving desired activities,

(3)   Obtaining information from sources unobstructed by interfering conditions,

(4)   Abilities of my systems to translate information presented by the "System",

(5)   Response ability of my systems to respond by mind and/or physical methods,

(6)   Relating ability of my system's vocabulary, understanding and background,

(7)   Interpreting ability for the responses from the requested information.

(8)   End of Program. Thank you.

Question 9 Safety Net Program

The Question 9 Safety Net Program: Is to become part of and work with all of my Programs for agreements and to be continually in effect until I choose to make changes. Considering all aspects related to my request and/or instructions associated with information, activities, or objectives, to please indicate the Lowest Level of Effectiveness for:

(1)   *Conditions necessary for the Dowsing or other "Systems" to achieve stated objectives,*

(2)   *Information completeness of instructions necessary to accomplish stated objectives,*

(3)   *Ability, conditions, and function for involved genes, energy fields, biological or etheric bodies, systems, and any other influencing factors for achieving stated objectives,*

(4)   *Time and Space conditions which include "when", "where", and "how long" statements,*

(5)   *Interference blocking ability from any source including personal conditioning and imprints,*

(6)   *Omitting necessary known and unknown conditions, influences, or aspects needed in the Programs, questions, requests or other areas not covered in this "System" to achieve objectives,*

(7)   *Results obtained for stated objectives.*

(8)   End of Program. Thank you.

Question 10 Completing Time Program

The Question 10 Completing Time Program: *is to become part of and work with all of my Programs or agreements and to be continually in effect until I choose to make changes. When requested, the "System" is to indicate completeness of the requested activities. The answer is to be indicated in numbers 0 through 100, where 0 equals none, progressing to 100, equaling complete. This is to be related to the requestor's indicated time in minutes, hours, days, or years. If no time is requested, it is to be in my perceived "now", or any other method or system the requestor may choose to use. End of Program. Thank you.*

For Best Results

Robin, do not try too hard and do not be too serious. Let it flow naturally. Relax and use your intuition. Let the information flow through you. You should always dowse with a loving heart and for the best good for yourself and others.

And Finally...

Take only what you wish from what I have offered and gently try to get hints from every dowser you meet or work with. There is a world of information out there and you will find it a wonderful, exciting, rewarding adventure!

Happy Dowsing,

Walt

Supplemental Materials by Walt Woods

Editor's note: The preceding sections of this book contain the information contained within the *Letter to Robin* booklet first published by Walt Woods. We have supplemented some additional information written by Walt in other booklets that were provided to us by Walt's family in order to provide you, the student, the most complete picture of what Walt would have presented in his dowsing classes.

In the next section of this text, we provide for you Walt's supplemental writings, including more detailed information on specific dowsing protocols, as well as his Teacher's Guide.

Ten Do's and Don'ts when Dowsing

1. **Dowsing is intended to provide you with objective information**. Do not decide what you want or believe the answer should be. Wait for the dowsing response, which you can then examine like a scientist. Ask further questions which might help you understand more clearly the meaning of the information if the answer is surprising. Especially when you may be investigating unhealthy or noxious energies, using a dowsing device avoids the need to physically sense or identify with these energies.

2. **Protect Yourself:** To avoid absorbing undesirable energies, simply Program or direct your mind to have a detached sensing attitude. Dialoguing with your pendulum as if it were a person is a way to keep your focus on the information you are seeking, rather than on undesirable energies that could interfere with your receiving objective answers. Such energies will focus on the pendulum rather than you.

3. **Word your questions carefully.** It seems that your Subconscious mind is very literal in its interpretation of questions and does not automatically pick up assumptions. For example, if you ask, "Does my car need gas?" The answer is YES *(your car uses air which is a gas)*. You *assumed* it knows you

were talking about the amount of gasoline in the gas tank, but that was not what you asked. I suspect that many apparent "wrong answers" really were correct to the literal interpretation of the question. **Make the question a definite request for information existing somewhere, and not for an opinion of the past, present or future.** If you do ask for an opinion, it needs to be compared to an agreed upon reference, such as, "As compared to..."

Incomplete Question Example

"Do I have enough money?"

The answer will be random because I did not specify what it is for or when. If instead, I asked, "Do I have enough money, in my pocket right now, for a $1 ice cream cone?" You could then get a very definite and accurate answer. Carefully plan your questions.

---

4. Useful questions request specific information on who, what, where and when.

5. **Life's Lessons and Restricted Areas:** Be very careful not to interfere with anyone's "Lessons in Life" or possibly their "Karma", or other unknown

areas, that are best left alone. Always ask your Dowsing System "May I, Can I. Should I…?" If the answer is NO, then tactful avoidance is advisable.

If your Dowsing System Says NO

If after asking the "May I, Can I, Should I…?" of your Dowsing system and you receive a "NO" response, it could be that the answer is not available at this time. Another possibility is that a "YES" answer now could interfere with a life lesson that is already in progress. In either case, simply drop the matter or try again later.

---

5. **Always respect personal privacy:** If we are tuning into the Subconscious, then we have access to a lot of information. Never (*except under very special circumstances*) dowse a person without their personal request. It's like looking at their personal diary without their permission. Some people know how to shield themselves, but most do not.

6. **Apparent Universal Law:** There seems to be a universal law of cause and effect, or "what you plant, you will reap", or an experience of "Karma", or "what you send out will somehow return to you", etc.

    - *Always dowse for the best good of others.*

    - *Never try to use this gift for evil or selfish gain.*

    - *Dowsing for your own or others' needs (not wants) is permitted.*

    - *Dowsing is a gift to cherish and share.*

7. **<u>DO NOT</u> diagnose or give medical advice of any kind!** Always advise anyone to seek appropriate medical advice if they think they have a problem.[20]

8. **Sharing with Others:** Gradually and discreetly share with those who want to know, but refrain from sharing with those it might frighten or offend. This is especially important when you are just learning yourself and may feel very excited about your discoveries and the possibilities for dowsing applications. It is wiser to be calm and objective, and thus more able to see how people you might begin talking with about dowsing are responding.

---

[20] CAUTION: At the time of this writing, under the U. S. Federal Pure Food, Drug, and Cosmetic Act of 1976, it is a violation of the law to attempt, in any way, to diagnose or treat any ailment or illness unless you are a medical doctor or other licensed health-care professional working under the most stringent State, AMA, and FDA approved conditions. Use good judgment and be cautious.

Are they responding with curiosity, boredom or fear? This awareness will help you judge better if now is an appropriate time to continue sharing.

9. **Keep your mind open to new ideas and look for ways to improve.** Be a life-long student, it will bring much excitement and joy to you and your friends. Don't let your personal feelings interfere with your looking and listening. You believe and feel the way you do is because of the time (epoch, period, era) of your birth, and its geographic and ethnic location. This is further influenced by your particular experiences, educational and religious background. Don't let your beliefs block examining new ideas. New information could improve good judgement.

10. **Keep it Simple:** Try to keep all aspects of your dowsing as simple as you can. Practice, practice, practice and enjoy your dowsing.

Water Dowsing Programs

The following tested Programs were especially designed for particular dowsing subjects and for use as a starting point. Use them to build from. Feel free to add, subtract, or customize them to your specific situations. Talk to experienced dowsers for ideas.

> **A Program is simply a mutually accepted, pre-established agreement and condition, between you and your Dowsing System.**

Remember when you are dowsing to always ask the, "May I, Can I, Should I...?" permission question any time the basic subject changes.

A Water Program

Before you start looking for water, you should install the following Water Program or some other type of instructions on which you and your Subconscious have agreed. This enables your Dowsing System to know exactly what you are looking for, and helps you get a prompt, correct answer.

This one, which I currently use is based on talking to many dowsers over the years, but it will probably change as I learn more in the future. If you are in classes, the instructors may have different versions that work well for them. Most Programs work well.

Once this Water Program is in your Subconscious, all you must do when dowsing, is ask simple water questions. Your Dowsing System will answer the questions, while referring to the pre-information and instructions that you put into the Water Program.

Note: The square brackets - [ ] - indicate flexible areas, such as [300] could be changed to [500] for a specific dowsing situation. Because of instructions you put into your Primary Program, it will automatically revert back to your original Water Program after you have completed the current search.

The three-step installation time is about 40 seconds.

1. **Get Permission.**
2. **Read Program.**
3. **Check to see if it has been properly installed.**

Letter to Robin

<u>Water Program:</u> *is to become part of and work with all of my dowsing Programs or agreements, and to be continually in effect until I choose to make changes.*

Depth: *The water is to be less than [300] feet deep.*

Minimum flow: *To be able to supply to the surface, from a well, a minimum of [3] gallons per minute.*

When: *To be able to supply the minimum amount of water specified, year-round once the well is created for a minimum of [10] years.*

Quality: *To be potable water (safe for humans to drink) and palatable to [me].*

Location: *Readily accessible to well-drilling equipment.*

Legal: *Meet the local requirements for a well-site location.*

End of Program. Thank you.

Note: When you ask a simple water dowsing question, all of the above is also in effect.

Some sample additional questions: *(May I, Can I, Should I question is asked each time.)*

1. *Is appropriate* **water available** *within [designate the area of interest]? (Note: All factors in the Water Program are in effect, so this is a YES or NO answer.)*

2. *Where is the **best place** to drill a well(s) [designate the area of interest], e.g. within 20 feet of the kitchen door]?*

For map dowsing, use a system to mark all water veins that fit the Program and best locations for well(s). (See Map Dowsing, page 91.)

For edge-of-property dowsing, where you cannot go onto the land to be checked for water, choose two accessible spots on the edge, marking them on a map of the property in question. The dowsing instrument will point towards the best location. Make straight lines in those directions from the selected spots on your map where they cross the location.

For on-sight dowsing, you can find the location by requesting the dowsing instrument to point in the direction of the best location, walking in that direction, continuing to hold the instrument, and asking it to stop when you reach the best well site. Mark it with a flag, stones or other object. It may also be helpful to indicate the direction of flow of the water vein(s) at that site by asking your dowsing instrument to point in that direction and mark it on the ground in an arrow shape with twigs or chalk paint.

Food (Substance) Program

Energy in its many forms is what dowsers work with all the time. Food is an obvious source of energy for human life. With dowsing, we can identify foods that can harm us and avoid consuming them. We can also, through The Dowsing System, request noxious energies in foods to be transformed into more beneficial ones, often with apparently amazing results.

Therefore, if food is an energy carrier, we could, and should, experiment with it by using focused intent and a pre-installed food Program.

Because contemporary the commercial farming practices of re-using the same soil each year, additional nitrogen, phosphorus, potassium, lime, and other compounds become necessary to stimulate normal plant growth. Large agricultural companies experience much pressure from their investors to produce economically profitable harvests. Adding these commercial fertilizers eventually leads to the depletion of the soil's natural fertility and consequently less nutritious food production.

The Food Chain (or Cycle)

In simple terms, the food cycle begins with above ground plants using photosynthesis to create sugar and other compounds to grow. Underground life creates organic matter and frees up soil minerals, and literally hundreds of different types of nutrients and compounds. Underground life needs sugar it cannot make on its own, and the above ground plants make sugar, but not what may be hundreds of other nutrients, trace minerals and other compounds essential for both our and their good health. Truly healthy plants have, over millions of years, developed very effective defense systems and relationships to protect themselves. But they require a healthy food chain to do so.

Healthy Soil

Soil Microbes
Ground Beetles
Bacteria
Microfungi
Protozoa
Nematodes
Earthworms
Millipedes
Spiders
Mites
Fungi

Nitrogen, Phosphorus, and Potassium in large amounts can be toxic to some underground life, breaking this food chain. Many insects in the food chain are attracted to old, weak, and malnourished plants, which can no longer defend themselves. The now malnourished plants need insecticides and other chemicals to protect themselves. These are the same plants we often need to eat

82

to survive. We now have urgent reasons for experimenting with dowsing both for the amount of nutrients in our food, and modifying the identified, and not yet identified harmful effects of these new chemicals to ensure optimum health.

The following is a suggested Program. Note that areas in [ ] are easily adjusted to suit your needs. The term "substance" is to mean any material, including food, drink, medications, etc. which I deliberately put in or on my body.

Substance Program: is to be continually available, to be a working part of other related Programs and Agreements and can be changed by the installer at any time. (So, when you request this Program to start, it will also include aspects of other installed Programs like the Overall Conditions Program below and the Primary Program, etc.)

Detection: Upon request to activate, the Dowsing System is to evaluate and indicate the worst condition detected, as caused by, or related to, anything going on, into or outside of my body.

Then when requested: the Dowsing System is to adjust, clear, modify, change, scramble, all the least desirable elements that are less than +10, including adjusting or transmuting minerals, vitamins, amino acids, antioxidants, pH's, and whatever else is needed for a complete functioning, balanced system that will create and maintain a healthy mind and body. It is also to promote easy, comfortable digestion and absorption, and make [my] entire body feel good and have abundant energy. This is to include, any one or combination of, all foods, drinks, air, and other influences that are known or unknown, which have or are going into the outside of [my] body and indicate progress.

Action Time: *When activated, this Program is to be in effect for [+/- 12 hours] and to be continuous until the requested modifications are completed.* **End of Program. Thank you."** [21] [22]

> **To be most effective, you may wish to mentally request this Program to activate each time you eat, drink, or take a supplement, etc. This helps to firmly establish these Programs. Notice that the Program is to be continually active until the requested adjustments are complete.**

---

[21] Suggestion: Each time you eat, drink, or take a supplement, etc., you should then, just for a second, recognize the Food Program. This will activate this and other attached Programs. That is all the time it takes for the "System" to respond to your pre-requested Programs. Next, imagine your food, in general, with thousands of rainbow lights (or white light, or your favorite energy enhancement color lights) of energy. This adds focused intent to your Programming. The combination of the two can often have amazing effects.

[22] Note about time: Some Programs have built-in activity time restraints. This is to make sure we stay aware and involved when we make a request. The "System" seems to not want us to permanently install and forget our Programs. We must stay involved and have the freedom to make changes at any time. All adjustments are in the "now". When something is adjusted, it may last for a very long time before it needs modifying. When this happens, we will need to rediscover the problem, which often has changed conditions, and make a new request for adjustments, corrections, or modifications.

Letter to Robin

Some sample questions:

If it is not appropriate to dowse in a particular situation (such as a holiday dinner with extended family) you might hold the pendulum under the table or train your finger to act as a pendulum.[23] First ask the "May I, Can I, Should I.." question, and upon a YES response, ask:

1. Is it better for my overall well-being that I not have any [ ] at this time?

2. Can the food value of [ ] to my body be increased to +10 by request at this time?

3. Is there any food on this table that could endanger my health today or cause an allergic reaction?

---

[23] Editor's note: You may also use Applied Kinesiology (aka Muscle Testing) to discretely obtain YES or NO responses to food choices. A simple application is to hold your middle finger against your thumb and apply pressure. When you ask the question, "Is this food item good for me to eat?" apply pressure against your thumb. If your finger breaks free, that indicates a NO response. If your thumb can hold onto your finger without breaking the circle, that indicates a YES response.

Practice Dowsing

Practice Water Dowsing

This is a good place to practice because your body is very sensitive to finding life-supporting water. You have already Programmed the *"Water Dowsing"* instructions and parameters, as well as all aspects of the *"Primary"* and *"Guidance" (or "May I, Can I, Should I…?) Programs* into your Dowsing System. You may have also had the experience of feeling, sensing, and seeing a positive personal water-sensing response in the classroom setting. It is now time to enjoy these reactions in an unknown location. Have fun!

Example Questions for Water Dowsing

Availability:

"Are there available well site(s) within the area I have designated?" This would be a YES or NO answer. Feel free to change the wording at any time.

Best Spot:

"Where is the best spot to drill a well, within the boundaries of my designated area, using the following instructions and responses?" Remember that all responses are based on your pre-programmed parameters, like maximum depth, etc.

If your dowsing reads on the nonbeneficial side, you may want to try this experiment:

Ask the Dowsing System if it "can and will do anything about [this] situation". If the answer is YES, ask the pendulum to be returned to swinging to the negative reading, and to please make appropriate corrections and indicate progress with the pendulum. Watch the pendulum swinging. It may move from the negative position to the balanced position, or possibly to the positive side. Use the swinging pendulum as a meter to indicate what is happening. Do not ask questions or interrupt it while it is working. Changes may sometimes be very quick and for differing amounts. Never underestimate the power of the Subconscious or other forces involved.

Dowsing On-Site Practice Using L Rods

If you are on or near the property you would like to dowse, ask your L Rod(s) to point in the direction you should walk towards to find the best location. Just follow their directions. They may take you around obstacles.

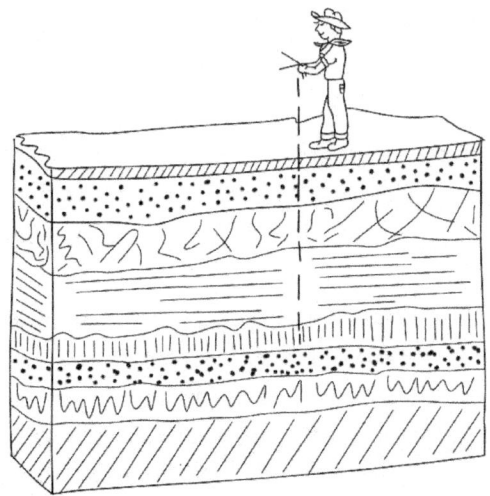

Water Dowsing

Location: Ask your L Rods to cross (for two L Rods) or quickly swing sideways (for one L Rod) when you are over the center of the greatest water flow for the best spot. There may be several good spots that you can find in the same way.

Number of Veins: Ask if there is more than one vein at this location within your pre-Programmed depth limitations. If YES, ask your L Rod(s) or pendulum to indicate a YES for each number you count and a NO when you go beyond the number of veins.

Depth: Ask for the depth of the first vein by asking your L Rod(s) or pendulum to indicate a YES as you count down the number of feet, or tens of feet, and to indicate a NO when you are beyond this vein. If there is more than one vein, do the same for each one.

> **Most dowsers advise that if you are doing this for someone else, only give approximate depths, and where you have added 10% or more to that number.**

Width of Water Source: Ask your L Rod(s) to indicate the outer edges, where there is a ¼ or 25% drop in flow compared to the greatest flow. This gives you an idea of the most usable width of this water source. You can also determine the distance from the top to the bottom of each individual vein in the same way you did for the depth.

Direction of Water Flow: Ask a single L Rod to point in the direction that the water is flowing. If there is more than one vein, you would check each one.

Available Water: Using the same counting method, you can determine the amount of water in gallons per minute (gal/min) from each vein, available to the surface.

> **Most dowsers advise that if you are doing this for someone else, and because of the many problems encountered in well-drilling, only give them your best guess and for one-half your indicated amount. If they get more water at less depth than you indicated, they will be very happy with you. If they get less, they may send you bad vibes or not refer you to others for the same work.**

Map Dowsing

Map Dowsing

Map Dowsing involves using a marking device of some kind, and a dowsing tool to locate water or other objects on a map.

*"**Map Dowsing Program:** is to become part of and work with all of my Programs or agreements, and to be in effect until I choose to make changes. When using a map or drawing, some type of dowsing device, and with or without an additional pointer or straight edge, the Dowsing System is to indicate when the pointer, straight edge, or dowsing device is indicating the present map represented location of the object, subject, or target specified by the dowser. **End of Program. Thank you.**"*

There are several common methods used for map dowsing. The first two below seem to be the basis for many systems. When you have carefully specified what you are looking for, and get a YES from asking "May I, Can I, Should I", choose one of the following methods:

Method 1: (Requires a dowsing device and a straight edge such as a ruler, paper, straight stick, etc.)

A. Slide a straight edge (ruler, paper, pencil, etc.) across a map or drawing, and ask the dowsing device to indicate when the straight edge meets the target.

B. When dowsing indicates that the straight edge is at the target, draw or site a line along the straight edge.

C. Turn your straight edge 90° and slide it across the map. Ask the dowsing device to indicate when the straight edge is at the target. Draw or site a line along the edge. **Your target will be located where your first and second lines cross.**

Method 2: (uses a pendulum)

Ask your pendulum to swing towards your chosen target. Ask the pendulum to spin when it reaches the target as you follow the pendulum's swinging direction.[24]

---

[24] Editor's note: The term "following the pendulum's swinging direction" can be challenging for beginning dowsers. As the pendulum swings, one side of the swing is going to feel stronger than the other. That is the "swinging direction" of your pendulum.

Method 3: (uses an L Rod)

Or ask an L Rod to point towards a target and hold that direction as you move. Ask the L Rod to turn crosswise when the target is reached and mark the spot where the L Rod turned crosswise.

You can use any of the above or invent your own. With practice, all methods, including your own will work fine. Have fun.

> **If you use a pendulum and chart, ask the pendulum to swing slightly to the left of YES and move closer to YES as you move your straight edge (or pencil) closer to the target (water vein, noxious zone, or object, etc.).**
>
> **YES is on target, and swinging to the right of YES is past the target.**

Over 100 Interesting Areas to Explore

If our dowsing system is tapping into our Subconscious, Higher Self, Superconscious, etc., then it may be possible that we can access to information about ourselves that is not available through what might be referred to as "normal means". This section has many examples of this type of information. It covers situations or conditions that may in some way influence our personal systems. It is divided roughly into four subdivisions, allowing you to go to topics of interest quickly.

There are four separate areas that the following Programs cover:

A. Energies and substances

B. Mind or spiritual influences

C. Chemical or biological areas

D. Things that cover what may have been missed in other areas or is in an area where you or I may not have an adequate knowledge or language.

A. Energies and Substances

Energy fields are everywhere! We are immersed in a sea of all kinds of energy. Electrical fields emanate from power systems, radio, TV, and radiation from the sun. Gamma radiation comes from the earth and from outer space. In addition, energy fields from underground water veins and fractures in the earth's crust are everywhere. The earth itself vibrates, has grid lines and a pulsing magnetic field, and there are many more known and unknown sources and types of energy fields. In the following discussions, we will be covering areas related to our external environment, our food, and internal body energies.

Noxious Energies

Noxious Zone

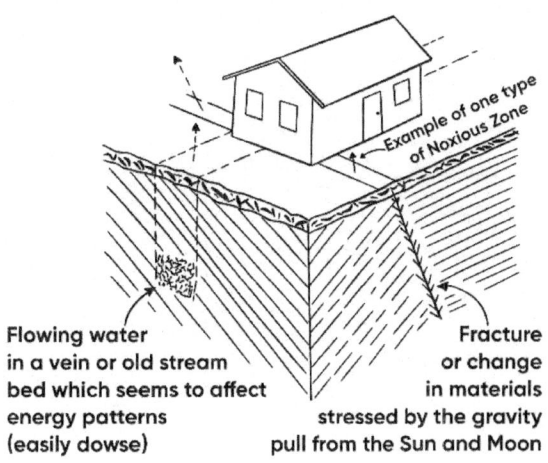

Noxious, or harmful energy fields come in an infinite number of types, strengths, and frequencies, and vary from location to location. Some of them may be important to our health, similar in some respects to trace minerals. Some are very low in strength, while others exist

Flowing water in a vein or old stream bed which seems to affect energy patterns (easily dowse)

Fracture or change in materials stressed by the gravity pull from the Sun and Moon

Example of one type of Noxious Zone

at a higher level, but well within our ability to handle them. Some of these energies seem to stimulate our defense, immune, and health systems beneficially, helping us to avoid deterioration from disuse. Others are strong enough that if we exceed what is our "safe time" in their presence, may become detrimental to us. These are sometimes called noxious energies, geo-pathic zones, irritation zones, detrimental energies, etc.

While noxious energies come from many sources, we will focus on two very important ones:

- **Fractures in the Earth's crust:** Fractures are created by the folding of the Earth's crust, they are quite numerous, and can be small to very long and deep (as in earthquake zones). They are constantly changing their influence, which can be weak to very strong, depending on the stress of the moving Earth's crust and the constantly changing gravity pull of the moon and sun. Noxious energies usually appear as a curtain of influence directly above the entire length of these fractures. Easily detected by scientific methods, they usually measure about three to four feet wide and go up for thousands of feet.

Geopathic Stress

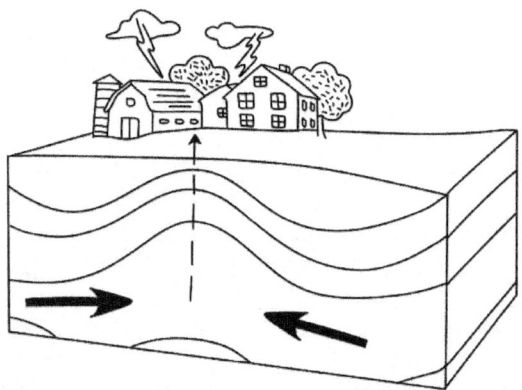

> **The Moon's gravity pulls the Earth's crust upward about two feet as it goes overhead each day. This creates a very long wave, like an ocean wave many miles long and wide and around two feet high at its center. The Sun has a gravity wave that is about twelve inches high at its center. The interplay of these two tremendous amounts of energy that varies over 28 days, and yearly, seems to stress the earth's crust in many ways. The result of this stretching and twisting can be detected by dowsing, and they have demonstrable good and bad erects on plants, insects and animals. Dowsing and experimentation have indicated that they may also affect humans.**

- **Moving Underground Water:** The energetic influence will usually be steady and directly above the water. It can be narrow to quite wide and vary in intensity depending on the width and configuration of the flowing water. The strength of this influence is primarily dependent on how much and how fast the water is moving, the type and shape of material it is flowing through, its depth, and other factors.

There are of course, numerous other influences for the Earth, outer space, and man-made events.

You should normally be able to dowse or otherwise detect the current location strength of your personal "safe time" at a specific location. This "safe time" varies from person to person, and can be from a few minutes to all day, depending on the existing conditions. One sure way to stay safe is to avoid staying in them longer than your determined "safe time". It just may be for some noxious energies, your system, for a time, is able to heal, handle, or repair faster than the non-beneficial effects can harm you and help you avoid disuse deterioration. What we sometimes classify as noxious energies are only harmful where we have an overdose such as too much sunlight can damage your skin or heat from a fire can burn you if you get too close to the flames.

Hormetic Curve

There are numerous ways in which noxious energies can be corrected or influenced. Either too little sunshine (as in seasonal affective disorder) or too much (as in sunburn or skin cancer) is harmful, while the right amount can provide beneficial Vitamin D absorption.

Noxious energies are very often only an overdose of what may be a beneficial energy. This principle can be applied to almost anything you can think of, and it is known in scientific circles as the "Hormetic Curve". You can find a dowsing-type *"Hormetic Chart"*, with instructions, in the *"Charts"* section of this book on page 145. Because energy fields may pose a possible danger to your body, the Subconscious is very sensitive to them, making it easy to dowse for information in this area.

Noxious Energies Program

Noxious Energies Program: is to become part of and work with all of my Programs or agreements, and to be continually in effect until I choose to make changes. The term, noxious energies, unless otherwise requested, is to mean, any form of energy, condition, zone, or situation that has, or could have a non-beneficial effect on any aspect of [my] total being, in a harmful, disrupting, or interfering way. This is not to include, unless otherwise requested, smoking, alcohol, drugs, medication, food, or drink that I have deliberately and knowingly put into or on [my] body. It is to include, but not limited to, the effect from magnetic or electromagnetic energies from zero to all frequencies, alpha, beta, and gamma energies, the influences from fractures or faults and underground water, and all man-made Earth or cosmic energies, gases, mind, psychic, and spiritual influences.

Questions for the Dowsing System for a designated area:

(a) ***"Are There"*** *noxious energies within the present and the previous [28] days, unless otherwise requested? If these conditions, in the [designated area] have not or could not accumulate to a non-beneficial level for [me], the System is to indicate a YES.*

(b) *For the* ***"Effects"*** *for [me], the System is to go into its effects indicating levels, including the levels of non-beneficial effects for the present and the previous [28] days.*

(c) *For the* ***"Safe Time"*** *question which is to mean: For the most beneficial time of day including the present and the previous [28] days, and for the maximum number of hours within that day where [my] body could handle this condition of non-beneficial effects. The indicating device should indicate the hours from near 0 to 24.*

(d) ***Adjustment:*** *The chosen system is to evaluate the area designated and indicates the levels involved. (This is a good time to make your request.) When adjustments are requested, the System is to adjust the noxious energies, within the designated area, in such a way that they are neutral or beneficial to any person, animal, plant, equipment, or other things seen or unseen, entering or occupying the designated area, and to make this continuous for a requested event time. (Like the life of a building, or as long as you are in a motel room, etc.) and the adjustment is not to otherwise cause non-beneficial effects.* ***End of Program. Thank you.***

The pendulum *(or dowsing tool)* **response:**

(a) To the *"Are There"* questions based on the previous [28] days. If the environmental conditions have not or could not accumulate to an interfering or damaging level for [me], the pendulum should go to NO *(indicating that [my] systems are able to heal, handle or repair faster than any damaging effects. This may be a good repair systems exercise to avoid disuse atrophy. Also, noxious energies are sometimes only good energies of which we had an overdose)*. If there are noxious energies that could accumulate to an interfering or damaging level, the pendulum should go to YES.

(b) To the **"Effects"** question, the pendulum should go to the worst negative level in Effects on any aspect of [my] total being, covering any time during the last [28] days.

(c) To the **"Safe Time"** question which is to mean: For the worst time of day during the last [28] days and for the maximum number of hours within that day where [my] body could handle this condition without harmful effects. The pendulum should go to a positive number from near 0 through 24. **End of Program. Thank you.**

You may temporarily substitute other names, times or conditions inside the [ ] by simply expressing your wishes to the Dowsing System while dowsing. The change will automatically revert back to the original Program after you finish dowsing in this area. This reversion back to the original Program is built into the Primary Program.

Working with Noxious Energies

Based on the Hormetic Curve, I would suggest that you not remove noxious energies, but instead request that they be altered, adjusted, or modified to be beneficial. This can be done using the *Noxious Energies Adjustment Program* below. If you have removed noxious energies, which may have also removed their beneficial effects, I would suggest that you ask your Dowsing System to go back in time and restore them to a beneficial level. This adjustment Program takes about 45 seconds to install. Be sure to (1) Get permission, (2) Read the Program, and (3) Check for acceptance.

*"This Noxious Energies Adjustment Program: is to be continually available, become part of, and work with, all of my related Programs or agreements, and can be changed by this installer at any time. When requested, the Dowsing System is to modify, change, or make adjustment to all the energies within an area that I have indicated, to be very beneficial for each human, plant, animal, piece of equipment, and others, seen and unseen, in, or entering this area. This is to be for the "Life" of the building or other selected "Event Time(s)", and not to cause any harm. **End of Program. Thank you.***

> Of all the areas where we use dowsing or other detecting methods, Noxious Energies may be one of the more important ones. We are asking our Subconscious or other sources to detect where there may be a less than beneficial influence within a designated area. It is an influence that, according to writers the world over, can sometimes be very detrimental. Because of the effect on the body, it seems to be very easy to detect these influences by dowsing or other methods.

How to Use the Noxious Energies Adjustment Program

The first thing I do while dowsing, is to designate an area I wish to work with. This is often a house and adjoining property. The next thing is to activate the Program. This is so the Dowsing System knows exactly what I wish done. You can do this mentally by requesting the Program by name or by using any part of the Program. It doesn't have to be exact, just so the Dowsing System knows which Program you want. I often say, *"Please modify all the energies in the area I have designated to be very beneficial to each human, plant, animal, piece of equipment, and others, seen or unseen, in, or entering this area, and to make this for the life of the building."*

Using The Hormetic Curve

This graph, or curve, represents substances and/or conditions in our environment. It can also be found in the *"Charts"* section of this book.

Hormetic Curve

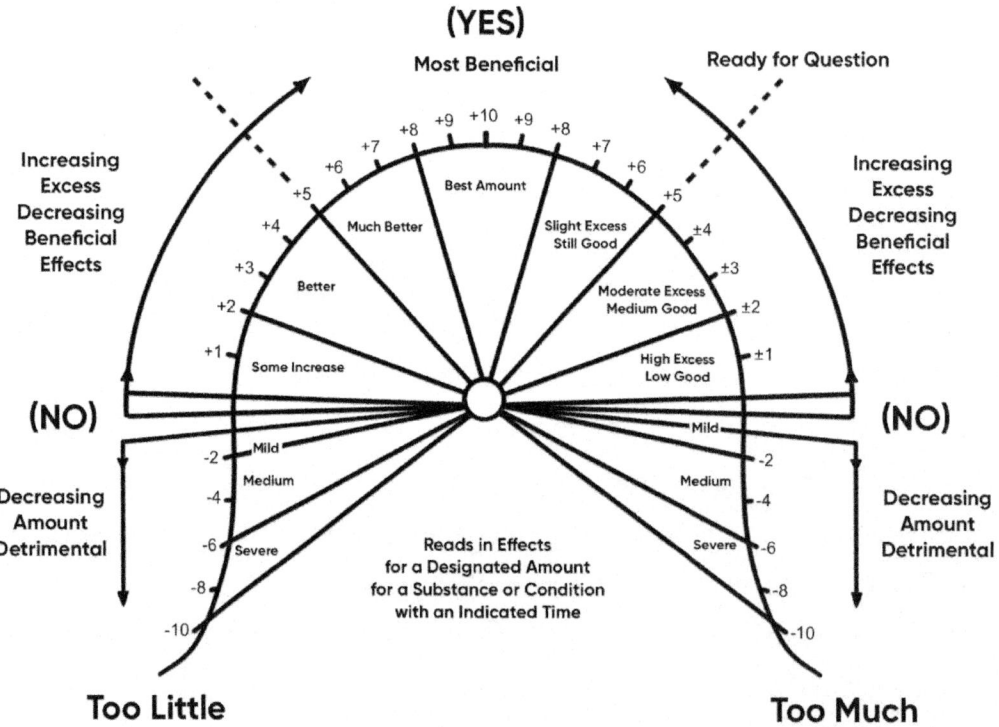

Letter to Robin

Example: Too little water (detrimental), proper amount (beneficial), too much (back to detrimental). The same is true for sunlight, exercise, air temperature, and nearly all Substances or Conditions. Check and see where you read for water consumption for the last 24 hours!

To use the *"Hormetic Curve Chart"*, hold your pendulum over the center of the chart and start it swinging toward "Ready for Question". This is the indicating half of the pendulum swing. Pretend you can't see the swing from the center away from the "Ready for Question". Then, ask your Dowsing System to indicate (swinging toward) the Effects of a Designated Amount and Time for a Substance or Condition. Either or both can be changed or adjusted for additional information.

Examples:

The amount of exercise (condition) for the last week (time)? If it reads (+2 Beneficial), this indicates that a little more would be good.

If I take [500 mg of...] (substance) each day (time)? If it reads +/- 4 moderate excess), this suggests that you might check if taking this every other day is preferable, or for an indicated decreased amount per day.

Conditions Program

Introduction

The first area to look at is the Programming of your Dowsing System. This informs the Dowsing System of what you are interested in, what parameters to use, and how to answer your questions. You should already have installed the *Primary Program* for this *Conditions Program* to build upon. The two Programs used together give the Dowsing System very thorough and mutually agreed upon conditions for exploring these interesting areas.

You can always add, delete, or change any part of any Program to satisfy your needs by following the three simple steps you have already learned (See page 41). If you make changes, it is a good idea to write them down so you will know what is in your programmed dowsing instructions.

The Conditions Program, once activated, requests your Dowsing System to detect, evaluate, and indicate the level of whatever is specified within the Program. Then you ask, it is to make adjustments, corrections, and modifications. The installation time is about 2 minutes.

Installation Instructions For the Conditions Program

The Overall Conditions Program: is to be continually available and be a working part of other related Programs and Agreements.

Response: is to be for desirable and non-desirable levels, YES, and NO, numbers, progress, and other requested information, action or indicators.

Time Period: [Starting with my "now" and including the previous 24 hours].

Reference Person: may be an average of all persons, in average health, of [my] [age] [gender] and [peer group], living within [200] miles. (If this reference person is placed at the center where a +10 is most desirable, and a -10 is least desirable (or use any other numbered scale which will allow you a simple reference point to compare [your] conditions, as less desirable (-), equal to, or better than (+), then, if undesirable, you can request adjustment of these conditions towards the most desirable level, usually on or near the +10.)

Request: (1) When requested, the "Dowsing System" is to indicate the worst condition based on a Reference Person and other interlocking Programs. (2) When requested, the "System" is to make adjustments, corrections, modifications, etc. adjusting them to the most beneficial level. This is to influence all conditions related to this and other Programs by modifying inside and outside influences, emotional energies, thought forms, situations, food, etc.

Rate: Corrections, adjustments, changes, and activities are to be at the highest appropriate rate with considerations for comfort and safety.

1. **Obtain permission:** With your pendulum swinging to Ready for Question, ask the Dowsing System the following questions:

   • *"May I, Can I, Should I, establish, change, or add Dowsing Conditions and Agreements or Programs which will be continually in effect until changed by me?"* If the answer is YES, you can then proceed to the second installation step (Step 2).

2. **Get permission to add the two questions 1 and 2** *(below):* Then read the questions followed by the statement, or other similar wording:

   • **1**: What is the level, in Effects, for [my] Overall Average Condition?

   • **2**: What is the level, in Effects, for [my] Most Harmful Conditions anywhere within my total being?

   • **Statement**: [Overall Average Condition] for 1, or [Most Harmful Condition] or [Worst Condition] for 2. This substitute wording is to automatically represent the entire question.

   • **End of Program. Thank you.**

This will act as a questions Program or mutual agreement for the questions going forward.

3. **Don't forget the Final Check:** Ask the Dowsing System:

- Are the Conditions or Changes acceptable as presented, being clear and non-contradictory, and open to change at my request? If the answer is YES, you are finished. If NO, use your pendulum to ask questions and try to determine why, then repeat until you get a YES.

Indication of Finished Results or Progress Program: (Two suggested approaches.)

1. Indicate what will be the finished result(s) for the request, then the time required. (You may wish to know if it's minutes, hours, or days.) or

2. Indicate progress by spinning, or other system, stopping when results are complete, or when request has been fully received to be delivered as appropriate.

End of Program. Thank you.

Once you have a mutual agreement with your Dowsing System on the parameters you wish to work with, you can then take a closer look at the next two requests asked for in order.

1. <u>Request for</u> <u>general, overall impression</u> of your total being or an averaging of everything.

In accordance with the entire Conditions Program, [you] would be compared to a person of average health, [your] age and peer group. This average person would show up on the dowsing circle as balanced with a straight up-and-down swinging motion of the pendulum. Hopefully your reading will be more positive by comparison.

2. <u>Zeroing in on specific areas</u>, as related to all aspects of your total being.

At this point, you can be as specific as you wish to be. For example, if you are investigating a specific dis-ease or condition you are currently dealing with, your comparison person or group would be other people who are also dealing with that specific dis-ease or condition. This person would also show up on the dowsing circle as balanced with a straight up-and-down swinging motion of the pendulum.

Receiving Results and Progress Information with your Dowsing Tool Program

1. Indicate the worst overall condition or individual conditions by swinging to numbers, spinning, or other methods.

2. Request corrections and indicate progress.

3. Request what the finished results are to be, and the time needed to complete the task. You may wish to know if it's minutes, hours, or days, etc.[25]

End of Program. Thank you.

---

[25] Editor's note: Sometimes, DNA changes may not be complete for months or years once the dowsing program has been initiated, but that varies according to the individual. Generally speaking, the amount of time it takes is appropriate for that individual depending on factors beyond our ability to discern. We can also request that tasks be completed without seeing the tool at work, and we can then check in later to confirm that the correction is taking place or that the correction is still in progress.

Chemical, Biological or Things We May Have Missed or Don't Understand

Interesting Areas to Explore on Yourself

You can use the **Multipurpose Circle Chart** for this section. This chart is also in the **Charts** section of this book on page 145.

1. With your pendulum swinging to Ready for Question, ask May I, Can I, Should I, dowse the *'Over 100 Interesting Areas'* on [myself]?

   • If the answer is YES, proceed to step 2.

   • If NO, trust its judgment. You may ask why.

2. With your pendulum swinging to "Ready for Question", ask Question 1 by either reading the entire question, or just saying *"What is [my] overall condition?"* or *"Overall condition"* or similar wording. (*When you installed the "Conditions Program" you built in this wording flexibility.*) The pendulum is programmed to move from Ready for Question to a beneficial or non-

beneficial position, reading in effects on the upper half of the dowsing circle. This will be comparing [you] to the average person in average health and of [your] age and peer group. Hopefully your dowsing will indicate a better or more positive reading than the vertical pendulum swing to Bal. *(Balanced)* for the average person.

3. Now return the pendulum to Ready for Question. Ask **2.** either in its entirety, or "What is [my] worst condition" or "Worst Condition" or similar words.

4. Start dowsing for each of the Conditions below and keep track of the level of each area tested. Read only the bold words. Your Subconscious is aware of everything you read into it while you were programming the Conditions Program. It only needs a clue as to what area you are interested in.

5. To save time, ask the Dowsing System to indicate which section the worst condition may be in, by using + numbers 1 through 4. Then search this section for the condition. Repeat step #2 looking for the next worst condition. If you don't find one, then you are done.

The pendulum is programmed to move to the effects of the **worst condition** involving any aspect of [your] total being.

- If the pendulum goes to the positive side, there is probably no further action necessary.

- If the pendulum goes to the non-beneficial, or less-than-average side, you will then have many options, some of which are below.

Examples

1. My overall condition? Example answer = +6

2. My worst condition? Example answer = -4

3. What section should I go to? Example answer = 1 (List 1 - see below)

4. Start down this section, one line at a time, asking for the effects, until you find the negative condition. Example: Meridians? Answer = +7

5. Aura? Answer = -4

6. When you have a negative answer, go to *"Possible Corrections"* (page 119).

7. What is my next worst condition? If the answer is (+) you are finished looking for the negative areas. If the answer is (-) then go back to step 3 (above) and determine which section to look in for the next negative area. Repeat until you find all the negative areas.

Multipurpose Circle Chart

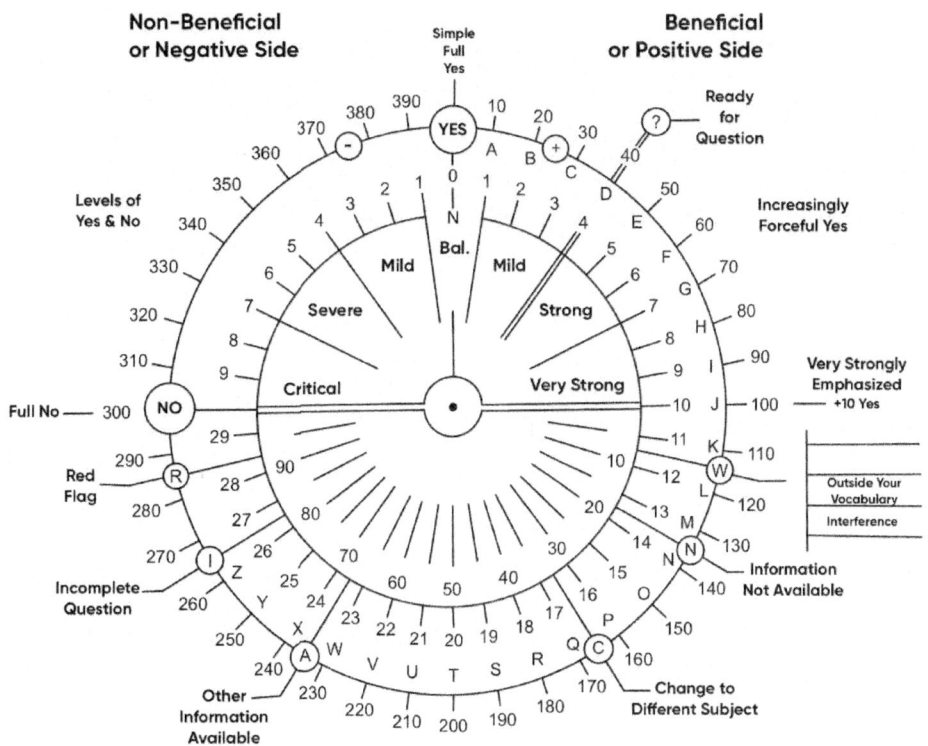

Personal Dowsing / Experimental Dowsing Research

As with all dowsing, Experimental Dowsing Research is not to be a substitute for medical advice. Feel free to ask questions at any time and dialogue for more information. Request an action, and if the action can and will be done. Ask how long it will take to complete the action. Unless otherwise requested, most questions will be related to the agreed-upon reference person. Unless otherwise requested, responses start with the "now" and include the past [24 hours].

1. "May I, Can I, Should I...?" YES, or NO

2. Outside Interference? -10 to 0

3. Overall Average Condition? -10 to +10

4. Specified Areas? -10 to +10

5. Worst Conditions? Anything less than +10

6. Areas Outside of My Concepts? -10 to +10

7. Progress Towards Specified Goals? 0 to 100%

8. Make Request. Check if it Can and Will? YES, or NO And later, for Time Needed to Complete Request? Minutes? Hours? Days? Years? You can ask these questions at any time.

Suggested Questions

1. What is the level of interfering conditions coming from outside [my] personal body? (Examples might be noxious energies, psychic influences, entities, etc. Use -10 to 0 scale and request corrections.)

2. What is the level of [my]: (Use -10 to 0 scale and request corrections.)

a. overall average condition, as compared to the reference person?

b. specific area(s) of interest, as compared to the reference person?[26]

c. worst conditions compared to the reference person? (Anything less than +10.)[27]

d. progress towards [my] specified goals? (Normally 0 to 100%.)

3. What is the level of other areas not covered, as compared to the reference person? (Areas outside of [my] vocabulary, awareness or concepts.)

---

[26] The answer will be specific.

[27] The System will start with the worst condition and start to make adjustments, while indicating its progress. If the adjustments require more than about 10 seconds, it will then arrange for the adjustments to be continually working in the background, while it starts working on the next condition. It will repeat this procedure in each area until it reaches +10. This would be a good time for you to ask how long, in minutes, hours, days, etc. it will take to complete any ongoing background adjustments. You can also dialog with The System for additional information. Dialoging is usually done by using the responses to YES, NO, and numbers, for questions asked.

Experimental Dowsing Chart

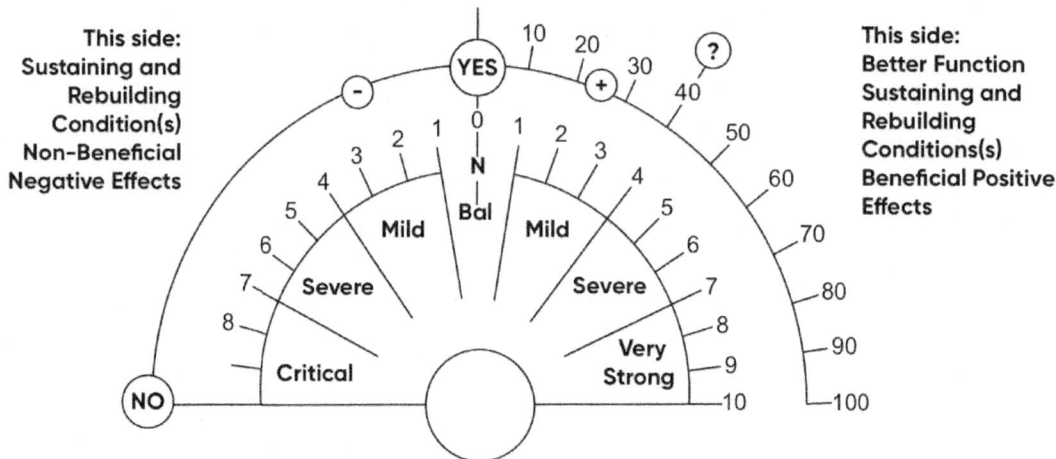

Directions: Unless otherwise requested, responses start in the "now" and include the previous [24 hours]. Feel free to change anything to fit your conditions or circumstances.

The Reference "Person": Questions normally, unless otherwise requested, are being compared to an agreed-upon reference person. This person is the grand average of all persons of [average health], [my] age, [gender], and [peer group], living within [200 miles]. If you use the **Experimental Dowsing Chart** above, the average person would be at the top center, with +10 being much better than the average person, and -10 indicating danger.

Possible Corrections to Detrimental Situations

Ask The Dowsing System if it can and will do anything about [this] situation. If the answer is YES, then ask the pendulum to return to swinging toward the negative reading, to please make appropriate corrections, and to indicate its progress with the pendulum. Watch the pendulum's swinging. It may move from the negative position to the balanced position, or possibly to the positive side. Use the swinging pendulum as a meter to indicate what is happening. Do not ask questions or interrupt it while it is working. Changes may sometimes be very quick and for differing amounts. Never underestimate the power of the Subconscious, mind, or other forces involved.

> **Remember, requests for situations to be changed is only experimental and to be used only on yourself. It is not meant to substitute for appropriate medical advice.**

Examples

If you are having a negative response for the Aura, *(like in a previous example)*, try the above corrections. Experiment to see what your dowsing reads after you finish.

If **Noxious Energies** are indicated, first try adding the following to the Noxious Energies Program, if you have not already done so.

Corrections Program

"Corrections are to be made by affecting the noxious energies in such a way that they will no longer have a negative effect on [me, my plants, animals and equipment]. This is to be for the entire [indicate the area you wish cleared] and for [the life of the building, or if I am involved, or any other appropriate request], and not to cause additional harm or interference to other persons, plants, animals or Mother Earth. This entire statement may be activated by words like: Please correct [indicate where, for whom, how long]

End of Program. Thank you."

After you add the Corrections Program above, recheck with your pendulum, or in the field, to see what has happened. Dowsing has indicated excellent results with this system. Many other systems work just as well, so use what works best for you.

Unusual Encounters

In rare instances, your dowsing might indicate the presence of undesirable negative influences by entities or other forces that we may or may not understand. These conditions may be local or from a distance or may be interfering or trying to take control.[28]

> **The words, "entity" and "forces" have very broad meanings and do not necessarily have a negative connotation.**

Possible Approach

Ask the Dowsing System if it will ask the "Medics" in the entity's world to please come and pick it or them up, give appropriate medical care, or take other appropriate action. Watch the pendulum for progress. You now have an idea of what to do.

---

[28] Editor's note: Many books have been written on this subject by dowsers who specialize in the investigation and clearing of negative entities and forces, some of which exist naturally as part of the landscape, and others that are the result of trauma both physically and metaphysically. The reader is invited to investigate areas of specific interest in the American Society of Dowsers bookstore as a more detailed discussion of this topic is beyond the scope of this book.

Conditions List to Check on Yourself

With your pendulum reading in Effects (Normal, Mild, Strong, etc.), use the two questions on any or all areas below. If you have not yet done so, you can add in the *"Conditions Program"* as well, below.

Two suggested questions after you ask, *"May I, Can I, Should I dowse Interesting areas on [myself]?"*

1: What is the level in Effects for [my] Overall Average Condition?

2: What is the level in Effects for [my] Most Harmful Conditions anywhere within [my] total being?

*"Conditions Program: is to become part of and work with all my dowsing Programs, and to be continually in effect until I choose to make changes. The response is to be for the **Level of Effects** or YES, or NO, on conditions, circumstances, situations, influences, and all other areas, as compared to the average person, in average health, of [my] age and peer group. These Effects may be singular or in combination, continuous or intermittent, for levels or amounts from subtle through very strong. They may be anywhere within [my] total being, covering the period [starting with my "now" and*

*including the previous 24 hours]. The response is to consider other influences or
conditions, which may not be listed, for each area."*

1. a _____ **MERIDIANS:** Acupuncture points and related energy fields

   b _____ **AURA:** Centering, Energy Levels, Leaks, Weakened Areas, Holes, Faults

   c _____ **COLOR BALANCE:** Chakras, Auras, Energy Fields, Infrared, Red, Orange,
   Yellow, Green, Blue, Violet, Ultraviolet

   d _____ **ENERGIES:** Love, Vital Forces, Life Energies, Prana, Chi, Yin/Yang,
   Emotional, Karma, Earth

   e _____ **NOXIOUS ENERGIES:** In the Home, Workplace, Other Living Quarters

   f _____ **VITAMINS:** C, B's, Pantothenic Acid, etc.

   g _____ **MINERALS:** Calcium and other allied minerals, etc.

   h _____ **BODY BALANCE:** Oxygen, Salts, Fluids, Sugars, Nutrition, Energies, Sleep,
   Rest

2. a _____ **MIND:** Energies, Force, Function, Controllability, Stress, Stability,
   Communications

   b _____ **EMOTIONAL:** Level, Hormone Influence, Environment, Substance Effect
   (food, medications, etc.)

   c _____ **ATTITUDE, IMAGES:** About Health, Life, People, Society, World, Self,
   Success, Failure

   d _____ **PATTERNS:** Mind Sets, Habits, Traits, Culture, Genetic, Ancestral Influences,
   Past Lives

   e _____ **NERVOUS SYSTEM:** Energies, Stress, Defects, Genetics

   f _____ **CLASHING:** Personalities, Vibrations, Oppression, Environment g _____ **SAPPING:** Of your Energies by any Method, System, Person, Force, or Entity

h _____ **PAST LIVES:** Reincarnation, Residual Effects, Entanglements, Attachments, Karma

I _____ **SPIRITUAL ENTITIES:** Possessing, Interfering, Aura, Vicinity, Often, Occasionally

j _____ **OTHER INFLUENCES:** Internal, External, Psychic, Mind, Familiars, Attachments, Entanglements, Sub-Physical, Astral, Spiritual, Entities, Karma, Environment

k _____ **SHIELDING:** Physical, Mental, Psychic, Astral, Spiritual, Aura and other types of shielding intended to protect us from undesirable influences, energies, forces, etc., and to allow for beneficial input.

3 a _____ **IONS and ELECTROLYTES:** Internal, External

b _____ **AMINO ACIDS:** Balance, Levels

c _____ **ACID/ALKALI:** Balance, Levels

d _____ **TOXINS:** Internal, External

e _____ **INFECTIONS:** All types, Physical, Astral, Spiritual, Psychic, Mind, and Others (fungi, yeast, bacteria, etc.)

f _____ **ALLERGIES:** From any cause or reason, Animal, Plant, Chemical, Mind, Psychic, etc.

g _____ **SYSTEMS:** Immune, Defense, Healing, Rebuilding, Hormone, Enzyme, Co-enzyme, Food Processing, Nutritional and Essence Conversion, Internal Communication Systems, and Others

h _____ **ORGANS:** Heart, Liver, Spleen, Pancreas, Bowel, Stomach, Lungs, Eyes, Hearing, Skin, Others

I _____ **PAIN:** Physical, Mental, Psychic, Spiritual, Astral, Warning

j _____ **PRESSURES:** Blood, Mechanical, Growths, Nerves

4 a _____ **OTHERS:** Areas known or unknown to me which are outside my vocabulary

Other names or times may be substituted inside the [ ] by simple request. **End of Program. Thank you."**

For possible changes using the Dowsing System, try asking the System what it can or will do. Remember that this information is Intuitive of Dowsing impressions NOT scientific data.

Walt Woods

Suggestions for Teaching Basic Concepts and Skills

The following course outline was originally developed for new instructors who were wondering how best to get started. As an instructor, your intent, of course, is to enhance the student's knowledge and understanding of dowsing, and to lay a good foundation upon which they can build accurately, easily and quickly, and provide appropriate practice using tools that gives them confidence and incentive to continue their education and build new skills as competent dowsers.

The following course outline could be used for a standard lecture time of one hour and forty-five minutes as a short introduction to dowsing. It could easily be expanded to a half- or full-day class by adding extra time for dowsing practice, interesting stories, questions, and field work. In planning your class, try to estimate how much time you wish to allot to each item on your list. Be aware that when you are teaching, the actual time it takes to explain a particular concept and answer questions from students will vary from class to class, so think beforehand of how you can shorten parts of your plan when other parts take longer to teach than you originally anticipated.

Letter to Robin

Over the years, experienced instructors have developed many successful courses to introduce new students to dowsing theory and practice. We know we can teach a person to use dowsing tools in about 20 minutes. We can also teach a person to plant some vegetables in about 20 minutes, but there is a lot more to dowsing and growing vegetables than that. Most gardeners and dowsers never stop learning.

Dowsing Course Outline

Introduction

Introduce yourself by telling your students the story of your own introduction to dowsing and how you use dowsing in your personal and/or professional life. Your goal is to establish rapport with your students so they can feel comfortable asking you questions and you can feel comfortable saying "I don't know" or "Let me look that up and I'll get back to you" when they ask you a question you didn't anticipate. Try to keep your personal story to less than five or ten minutes.

Give a short history of dowsing - Found on cave drawings and mines in the 1700's. Talk about dowsing organizations, chapters, groups, and publications. Explain the many areas where dowsing can be used, as in well-finding, archaeology, lost systems, etc. (See Appendix C: A Brief History of Dowsing, on page 162)

Getting Started

It is very important to always start your presentation on a positive, successful note. Hard science has shown that a negative experience during the first three minutes in a new subject area has virtually permanent effects. This may have something to do with our survival instincts. It may relate to our specifically remembering negative experiences for defense reasons.[29] On the other hand, a pleasant introduction could open students to understanding dowsing easily and developing their skills quickly.[30]

What is Dowsing?

You might explain that dowsing is using a device or some sensing method, to obtain information which appears to come from many contributing sources. (Refer to the Chapter "Dowsing Basics" starting on page 16 of this text.)

---

[29] Research by Dr. M. Sunnafrank, Professor of Communications, University of Minnesota, and many others.

[30] Examples of "ice-breaker" exercises include: Laughter Yoga, a brief guided meditation, stretching, or anything else that involves movement or promotes a fun, casual atmosphere.

Who Can Dowse?

Little kids learn to dowse quickly and easily. They don't waste any energy worrying that they might not be able to succeed at this new opportunity to develop a very useful life skill. All of us retain our inner, open, playful inner child, even as we become adults. Tapping into positive childhood experience can help us relax and discard any current fears of failure that could make it harder for us to learn to dowse now.

Introduction to Standard Dowsing Tools

Name and distribute each of the basic dowsing tools and show the students how to hold each tool and how it works with their bioenergetic field.

Be sure to provide plenty of time for students to practice with each tool immediately after your demonstration.

Introduction to Dowsing Charts:

Dowsing charts can be any size or shape. They can be created for any situation you wish to investigate with a dowsing tool.

Use the charts in this book, but also feel free to provide examples of other chart types the students can learn about through the ASD bookstore.

Chart Types

+ **Cross**

⊕ **Circle or Semicircle**

▭ **Ruler or Flat-line Chart**

The hand chart

How to Use Dowsing Tools

Have the students practice making the pendulum swing to Ready for Question. See an explanation on how to make it go and keep it going on page 146. After a short time, and while the pendulum is still swinging, have it work its way to the YES and then to the NO. Help them if necessary. Have them practice until, when they request it, it seems to move to YES or NO on its own.

Demonstrate how to hold and use other tools of your choice, like the L Rod, Y Rod, Bobber, and others. Let them experience and practice indicating the Ready for Question and the YES and NO. Save the other information on dowsing until after you have presented the programming and how to ask the dowsing questions.

Introduction to Programming

Explain the necessity of letting your Subconscious know what you want it to do. It is no different than when you use your mind and Subconscious to write a letter. You must tell your Subconscious what you want in the letter for it to use your pre-programmed bio-electrical muscle system to write the words.

If you don't inform your Subconscious about what you want, and how it is to respond, it doesn't know and will only guess at what you probably want, sometimes with questionable accuracy. (The reason for this is clearly explained in the *Questions* section.)

Three Steps to Programming

Installing a Program is very easy, just like training your mind to read musical notes and your Subconscious bio-electrical muscle system to move your fingers.

Your students need to inform the Subconscious how to respond and what to consider by reading Programs prepared for installation.

The Three-Step System

1) **Get Permission**
2) **Read in prepared Program instructions**
3) **Check if installation is complete**

Installing Programs

Get permission to install Programs. Your and the student's pendulums should now be continually swinging to the YES.

Have your students practice moving their swinging pendulums to one side into their peripheral vision (seeing it out of the corner of their eye). This seems to have a kind of post-hypnotic effect while you are reading in a prepared Program. This installation is intended to be permanent in your Subconscious, until the installer and only the installer, chooses to change it. You are programming your Subconscious and your Dowsing System, not the tool. You do not have to repeat Programs each time your dowse: getting a YES on Ready to Dowse reminds you and your Subconscious that your installed Programs are already in place.

Three Example Programs that you could help the students install:

These are easy Programs to install, and they will give the student's Subconscious and the Dowsing System some pre-arranged instructions to work from. Read them out loud to your class. As your class listens, all pendulums are swinging in the YES position.

1. **Primary or Foundation Program**: This Program is the foundation for all other Programs to build on. Installation time is about 2 minutes and 45 seconds. (See page 46.)

2. **Guidance or the "May I, Can I, Should I...?" Program**: Installation is about 45 seconds. (See page 46.)

3. **Water Program**: Installation time is about 40 seconds. (See page 77.)

Asking Dowsing Questions

Explain the importance of carefully worded questions that are literally correct. Students should not expect the Subconscious or Dowsing System to automatically know what their intent is if their mind is running a mile a minute with all kinds of conflicting thoughts. This is especially true when dowsing questions are not stated clearly with focused intent.

Practicing Dowsing

Once the students have had some good experiences in known areas, it is time for them to have fun experimenting in unknown areas.

See some suggested water dowsing questions on page 77. Practicing with these will help students become comfortable using their L Rods and other tools. You may prefer to guide practice in other areas than water dowsing, especially if your own area of expertise is in a different dowsing field.

Word Definitions

Some words used throughout this book may need a specific definition assigned to them. Bring up definitions only if they ask, or if you choose to say something about them.[31]

Dowsing System

Noxious Energies

Subconscious

Superconscious

Spirit Guides or Guardian Angels

Entities

Any other words you might wish to define.

Other Areas

In an all-day class, and if they are doing well, it may be a good time to introduce students to some simple *"Map Dowsing"* procedures to have fun

---

[31] You may refer your students to the list on pages 14 and 16 but be careful to not provide too much detailed information at once as it could be overwhelming to your students.

with but be careful to not overwhelm your students with too much information. It is better that the beginning student becomes confident and consistent with simple YES/NO questions than working to train them to become professional dowsers!

Suggestions for the First-Time Dowsing Teacher

Introduction

It is not unusual for people to be a bit apprehensive when they talk to a group, especially for the first time. This is sometimes called "stage fright". The following are some suggestions not only to make you more comfortable, but also to make this a fun and exciting adventure for both of you and fellow dowsers.

Be Yourself

If a friend came up to you and said, "Tell me about dowsing," what would you do? Simple! You would have a great time sharing! What if three or four friends came up and asked the same question? It could even be more fun because of the collective interest, excitement, and added questions.

Each of your students is an individual, and, just like your friend or group of friends, they are interested, or they would not have come to your presentation. It doesn't matter if it is one person or more, see them with the same fun and excitement with which you would see your friends. The audience senses this energy, and they respond to and enjoy it just like your friends do.

Sometimes a new speaker gets self-conscious and wonders what to do with their hands. The answer is simple. Forget about them and use your hands and body language just as you normally do. Your hands, arms, and body language add a lot to your words. Just be your normal self. Think of yourself as being with friends to have a good time. If you can maintain this attitude, you will be fine.

Use An Easily Visible Course Outline

It is very comforting if you have a list of main subjects you wish to cover, similar to the one in this book, to glance at from time to time. You will feel more confident that you can remember what you have already covered and include all the topics you intend to explore with your students.[32]

---

[32] Your list could be large and posted for everyone to read, you could put each main topic on a slide of a PowerPoint presentation that's projected on a screen, or you could put each topic onto a set of cards on a podium or handy table where you can easily refer to them. Do what feels most comfortable for you that won't be a distraction for you or your students.

Make Sure Your Audience Can Hear You

The following tips will help you get your message across in a pleasant way for both you and your audience of fellow dowsers. If you can't hear what a speaker says, it's no fun being in an audience. Talk loudly enough so the people three quarters of the way back in the room can hear you easily. Ask them if they can hear you and invite them to move closer to the front if they can't. Everyone wants to hear what you are sharing; that's why they came!

Some people can easily project their voice and be heard and understood in a room that holds up to about 25 or 30 people. Other people just have a soft voice that is difficult for people to hear without enhancement. As a general rule, if you have more than 20 students in the room and you do not have a naturally loud voice, you should use some type of audio system.

Tips On Using a Microphone Effectively

Always treat a microphone as a friend that is helping you share in a pleasant and enjoyable way. If you are using a hand-held or fixed microphone, do two things.

1. Keep the same distance and position from your mouth to the microphone constant.[33]

2. Listen to the volume of your voice coming from the speakers. You can tell if it is too loud or soft. If you forget about the position of the microphone and your volume you will lose your audience. Your prime purpose is to share your information. If they can't hear it, they won't get it.

3. If, however, you use a lapel mike clipped to your clothes, about 6 to 8 inches from your mouth, (about a stretched hand-width) you can basically forget about the microphone and just give your talk.[34]

Find and Use a Good Talking Speed

The average conversation is about 125 words per minute. You may know from personal experience that some people talk so fast that you have trouble comprehending an idea before they are onto another subject, and you never really catch up. On the other hand, if they talk too slowly, your mind wanders, and you can get sidetracked. In both cases you often miss their point.

---

[33] Editor's note: Practice at home beforehand, turning your whole body, keeping your arm in a comfortable, constant right-angle position, holding a dummy microphone until this action feels normal.

[34] Editor's note: Some audio systems don't allow you to hear or "monitor" your voice volume because the audio system automatically adjusts the volume to a comfortable level for all areas of the room. You may find yourself speaking too loudly if you're accustomed to listening for your echo. Some audio systems have a half-second delay to account for the speed of sound in large auditoriums. Just remember to speak as normally and naturally as possible and learn to ignore distracting auditory cues if they are part of your audio system operating normally.

Testing your own natural speed is simple. Count out 125 words in a newspaper or book and read them out loud as if talking to a person. While doing this, time yourself with a stopwatch. If you take between 45 seconds to a minute and 15 seconds, you are fine. If you are too slow or too fast, be aware of this, and try to modify your speed.[35]

How People Learn

All people learn in four primary ways: 1. Listening, 2. Reading, 3. Watching (demonstration), and 4. Doing (hands-on). For dowsers, we could add a 5th one, Sensing or Intuiting. Each person obtains information at different levels from each area. For example, one person may get most of their information from hands-on experience with only 10% listening, while another may get 60% of their information from reading, etc. When teaching, you should try to present your material in several different sensory ways.

For example, if you are explaining for the first time about the pendulum, you would **say** what it is, **define** it, **write** the name on a black board, whiteboard, flip chart, or projector. **Hold your pendulum** up for all to see. Have each person hold one in their **own** hand if possible. Then continue to explain about

---

[35] Editor's note: older people with hearing problems may prefer a slowing talking speed than average and will appreciate your efforts to speak more slowly than what you would consider to be a normal talking speed.

using the pendulum, inviting the students to copy your actions with it as you talk.

Example: Teaching Map Dowsing Using Multi-Sensory Methods

In a stand-up presentation with only talking, physiologists tell us that the average person can remember about 5% of the details after a week. What details could you tell me about a "talking heads" documentary you saw on TV a week ago?[36]

If you are explaining Map Dowsing in a classroom, you might use the following general approach: Draw a large square on a blackboard or flip chart. Make sure students can see your drawing easily. Designate it as a virtual fenced-in field. Have the students create a comparable virtual field on a piece of paper, which they already have available where they are seated. (Ask the Dowsing System to create a virtual water vein that curves somewhere in your virtual field.) Next, using your dowsing tool, move your chalk or pen across the drawing until the dowsing tool indicates you are on the center line of the water vein. Mark the spot and repeat several times. Ask the Dowsing System to create an identical virtual curving water vein at the appropriate scale for size

---

[36] Editor's note: At the time this was written, most documentary films consisted of a series of interview and were generally presented in a "lecture" format. Documentaries today are generally higher quality, which involve more of the senses, making them more entertaining and thus, viewers find them more memorable.

somewhere in each student's virtual fenced field. Now have the students do the same thing on their drawing after watching you do it. Do this several times until they have several dots along the center line of their virtual water vein.

Next, have the students watch you connect the dots until you have a water vein center line. Ask them to connect their own dots to form water vein centerlines.

Do the curving lines look like the large one you made? If not, why could that be? Remember, practice makes perfect. We learn by trying new things until they become easy to do.

Having the students follow you doing the same thing reinforces their memory of what you did. They saw what you did, heard your explanation, and they had a hands-on experience. You have provided them with an excellent memorable learning experience.

Continue your multi-sensory approach in the field. For example, have your students imitate you after you find a water source outdoors. After practicing a few times in a known area, they will enjoy practicing in an unknown area, moving confidently to independent dowsing with no fear of making mistakes.

Conclusion

Teaching dowsing can be a great pleasure to both you and your students. Just be yourself and enjoy this wonderful opportunity to share and inspire.

Appendix A: The Charts

The YES/NO Chart

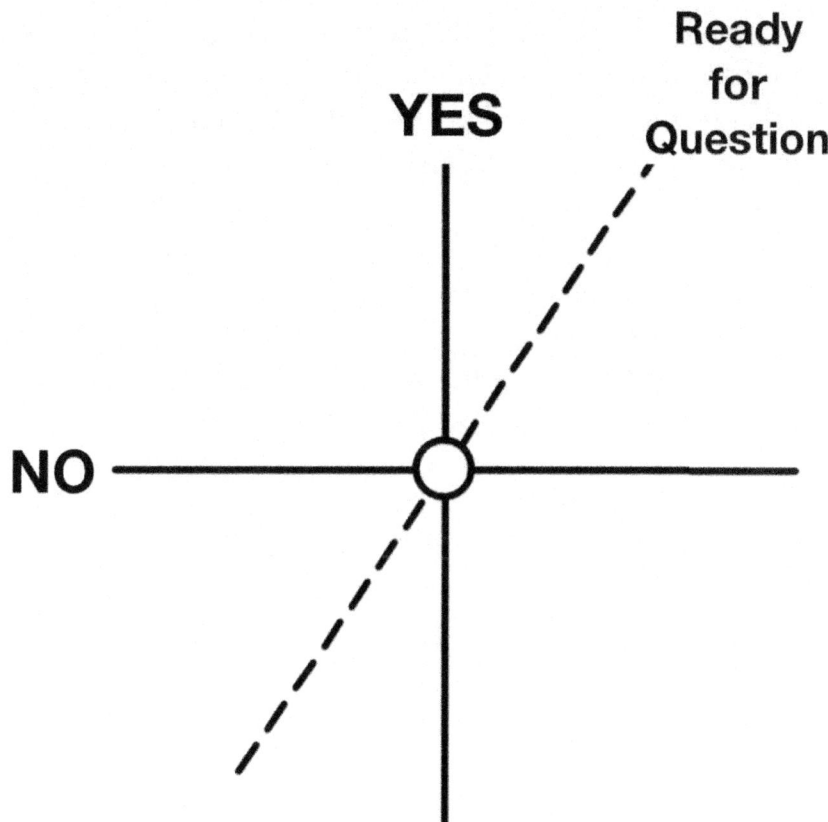

Teaching Your Pendulum to Work with the YES / NO Chart
Hang your pendulum directly over the center of the cross point, or the bottom of the half circle, and deliberately start the pendulum swinging toward Ready for Question.

Physically make it go, as this is to start training your Subconscious bioelectrical muscle system. If it stops swinging, just start it up again, helping your muscles to remember this new action.

Now, while you have it swinging to Ready for Question, help it work its way to the YES and then back to Ready for Question. Now do the same thing for NO. Each time, you will be deliberately helping to keep the pendulum swinging, training your muscles to swing the pendulum automatically in the future.

Practice these maneuvers several times.

Then begin to ask questions to which you already know the answer. Keep your questions simple in order to avoid unclear or nuanced answers.

When you see that the pendulum is providing consistent results, begin to ask questions where the answer is unknown to you, but you can easily discover the answer by other means. For example, you may ask, "Is my spouse at home right now?" After you receive your answer from the pendulum, you can call them on the phone to confirm their location. Or you can ask, "Is it raining outside?" and then look out the window.

When you are feeling confident that you are receiving consistent answers, you may move on to the more advanced dowsing charts.

The Hormetic Curve Chart

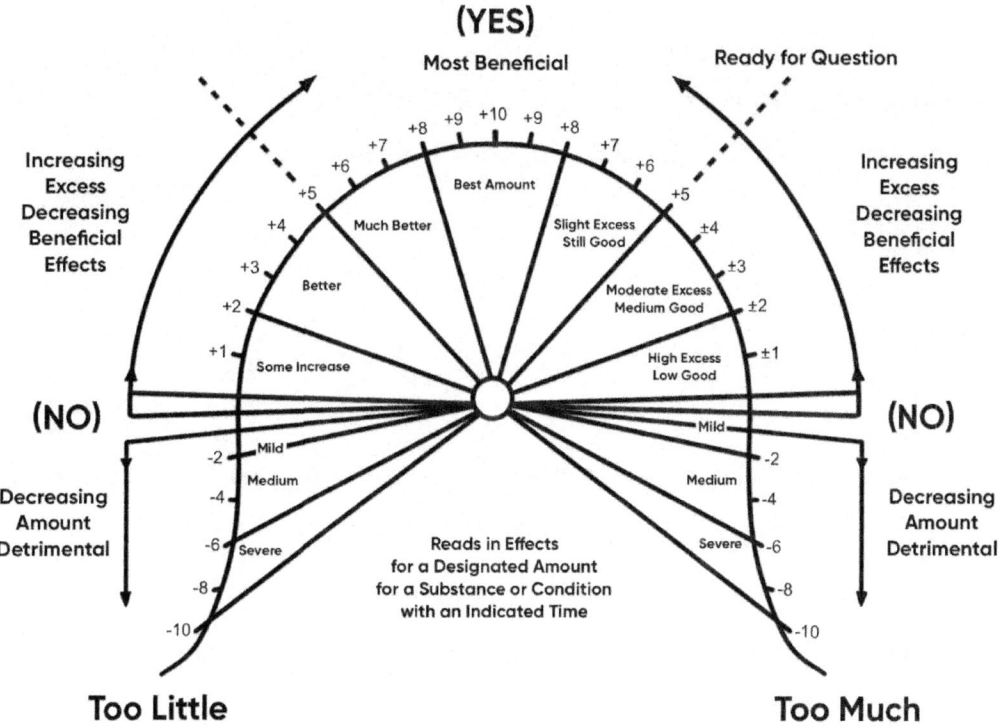

The Hormetic Curve Chart represents something we are all familiar with, where neither too much nor too little is beneficial. It is the chart of choice if you choose to dowse for Substances and Conditions. (See page 123 for a handy list you can use.) For example, too little water is detrimental to your health. A proper amount is beneficial, but too much water is again detrimental. The same is true for sunlight, exercise, air temperature, trace minerals, vitamins, and nearly all substances or conditions.

Instructions

Ask your "Dowsing System" to indicate the Effect of an Amount for a Substance or Condition as related to a specified Time (hours, days, months, etc.). You can also change the amount and/or time to obtain additional information.

Examples

(1)   The amount of exercise (condition) for the last week? (Time) If it reads (+2/+10 Beneficial), this indicates that a little more would be good.

(2)   If I take [500mg] of … [Substance] each day (time), what would be the effect? If it reads (+/-4 Moderate Excess), this suggests that you could ask about every other day, or an indicated lesser amount per day, to see what it reads.

The Multipurpose Circle Chart

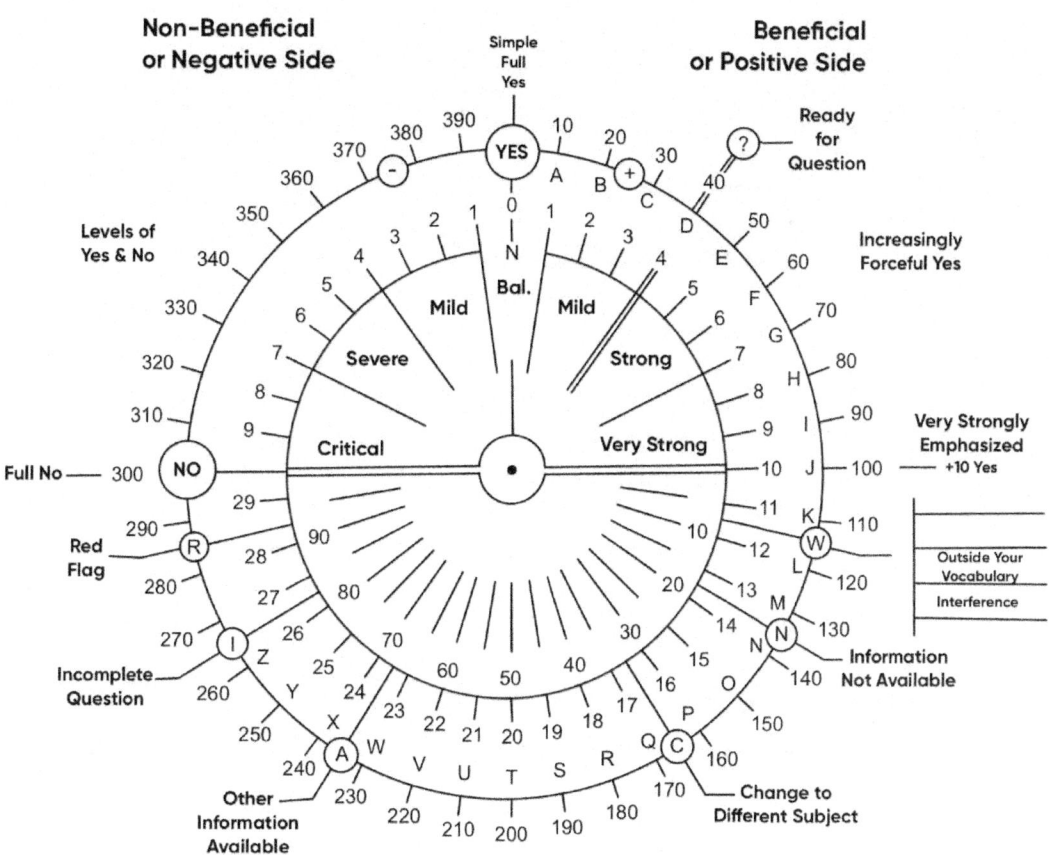

Multipurpose Circle Chart

This Chart is designed to allow you to dowse most situations by using a pendulum or any suitable dowsing tool. You can also receive guidance from The Dowsing System independently being able to indicate additional information you might like to consider or explore. You can just ask, "Any special guidance?" and the pendulum will swing to the appropriate indicator(s).[37]

The Dowsing System's own helpful guidance categories are marked as follows, from the left:

R	**Red Flag**
I	**Incomplete Question**
A	**Other Information Available**
C	**Change to Different Subject**
N	**Information Not Available**
W	**Whatever other categories it is willing to add**

This Multipurpose Circle chart combines aspects of all the other charts in this book and is designed to provide you with the broadest range of possible answers to your questions. This chart is unique as it offers further

---

[37] Editor's note: See the lower part of the chart and the six labeled further guidance indicators. You may add extra categories of your own on the W indicator, which is on the upper right of the lower chart upon request of your Dowsing System.

communication with your Dowsing System that reveals other areas of investigation beyond your original question.

Examples

(1)   The amount of exercise (condition) for the last week (time)? If it reads (+2 Beneficial), this indicates that a little more would be good. However, if it reads "Incomplete Question", the System is informing you that you need to refine or restate your question to obtain the information you are looking for.

(2)   If I take [500mg] of … [substance] each day (time), what would be the effect? If it reads (+/-4 Moderate Excess), this may indicate that you could ask about every other day, or an indicated lesser amount per day, to see what it reads. However, if it reads "Other Information Available", this may indicate that an additional substance needs to be added to increase the effectiveness of the substance in question.

Requests for Adjustments and Corrections

If you get a negative or undesirable reading, ask the System if it can and will make corrections. If YES, ask the System to make progressive adjustments, modifications, corrections, or changes towards the highest appropriate positive levels.[38] [39]

---

[38] This will usually be at or near +10.

[39] Editor's note: The word, "appropriate" is a very useful word in dowsing for changes. Dowsers may not know exactly what the most beneficial change for themselves is or another individual, but the Dowsing System does and can be relied upon to do the "appropriate" change.

The Personal Dowsing Chart

Personal Dowsing Chart

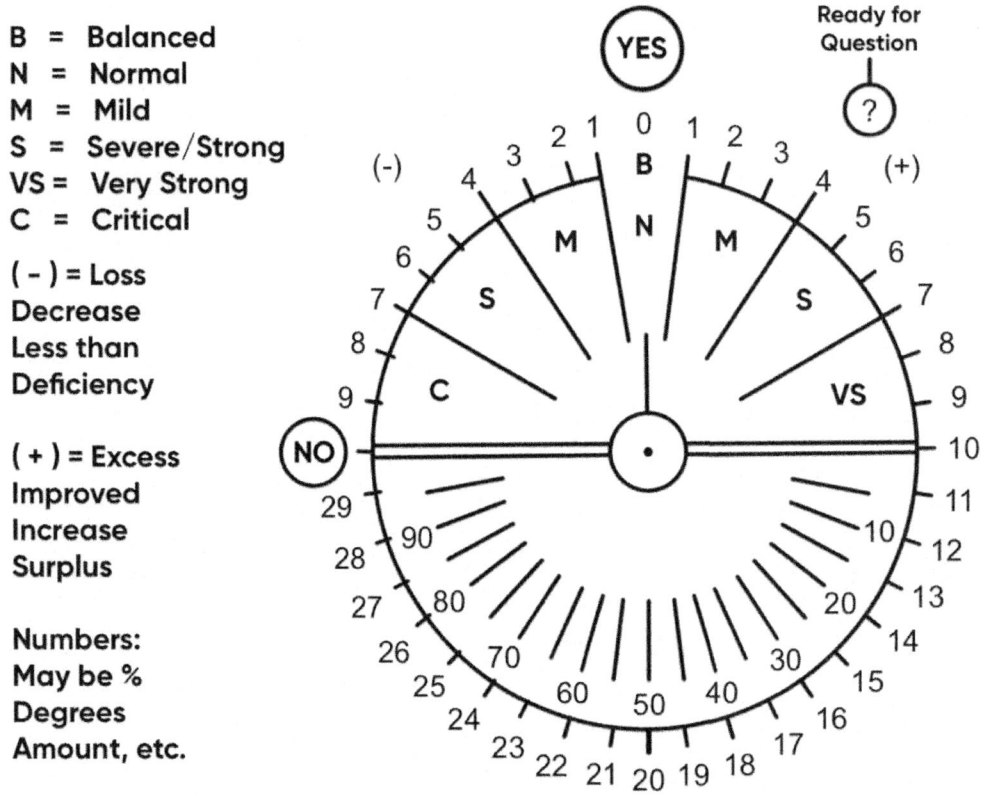

B = Balanced
N = Normal
M = Mild
S = Severe/Strong
VS = Very Strong
C = Critical

(–) = Loss
Decrease
Less than
Deficiency

(+) = Excess
Improved
Increase
Surplus

Numbers:
May be %
Degrees
Amount, etc.

Note: The significance of the alphabet letters inside the upper half of the chart is explained to the left of the circular chart. The inside numbers of the lower half of the chart provide percentage answers. The upper half outside numbers allow you to rate positive or negative results on a scale of 1-10. The numbers from the top (0) around the circle clockwise gives you a scale of 1-30, which is often useful for time (hours, day, etc.).

Purpose of the Personal Dowsing Chart

The intention of this chart is to provide the user with an indication of greater than or less than an established reference point, generally pertaining to personal health or life choices.

Establishing a Reference Point

Before you begin to use this chart, you must establish a reference point. For example, if you want to ask a question regarding your personal health, your reference point may be the average health of a person of your own age and activity level.

If, for example, you want to know if your current vitamin C levels are adequate for maintaining your health, you must first ask your pendulum to calibrate to the average vitamin C level for healthy adults of your age and gender. The swing of the pendulum should rest at the "B" or "Balanced" position.

Then you may ask your question regarding your own vitamin C levels. If it indicates a minus 3 (-M or Mildly Non-Beneficial), then you might ask what the effect would be if you took 500 milligrams of vitamin C. It would probably go to +3 or +4 (+M or Mildly Beneficial). You may then ask what would happen if you took 100,000 milligrams of vitamin C. It would probably go to minus 5 (-S or Severely Non-Beneficial).

Choosing Areas to Explore

There are many areas that you might investigate playfully. Pick ones that you are not emotionally concerned with, or for which you have prior definite knowledge of the answer. Also, keep in mind that your answer is not intended to be a medical diagnosis. If you are concerned about a result you receive from your dowsing, you should consult a qualified health professional.[40]

---

[40] Editor's note from Joan: It is not necessary to mention to your doctor that your dowsing is what raised your concern about a medical condition you are facing unless you choose to do so as some licensed health care professionals value dowsed data, while others might not understand how dowsing works and disregard or choose to dismiss it. In my own dowsing experience, a friend of mine was faced with severe medical problems that her doctors had not been able to diagnose. She asked me to dowse her condition using a chart from a well-known dowser from Boulder, Colorado. I dowsed that the cause of her current difficulty was the result of liver flukes, contracted from eating infested pork that was not fully cooked, which was a very unusual diagnosis for a person living in Canada. However, she worked as a travel agent and had visited several countries with much warmer climates where this type of infection was more commonplace. We worked together to phrase the inquiry for her doctor so that they could authorize a test for liver flukes given the fact that she recently traveled to several warm countries. The doctor authorized the test, and after she tested positive, she was then successfully treated for her condition while leaving out the fact that our original hypothesis was derived through dowsing.

The Experimental Dowsing Chart

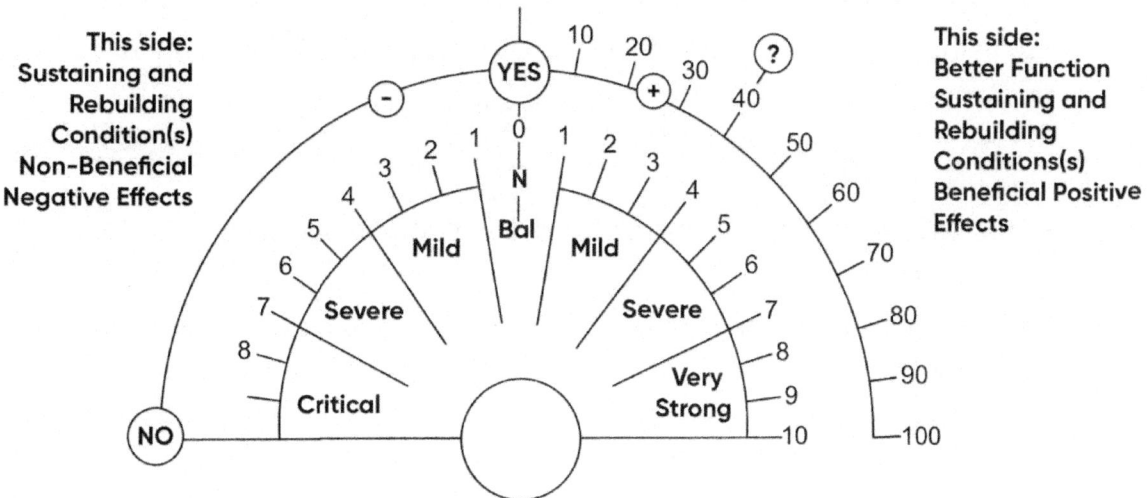

This side:
Sustaining and
Rebuilding
Condition(s)
Non-Beneficial
Negative Effects

This side:
Better Function
Sustaining and
Rebuilding
Conditions(s)
Beneficial Positive
Effects

Purpose of the Experimental Dowsing Chart

This chart is designed to allow you to dowse specific choice points primarily for yourself. This dowsing chart was intended to be used only on yourself to practice dowsing for experimental areas in your own person where the results may vary between individuals.

Define the "Reference Person"

Normally, questions are being compared to an agreed-upon reference person unless otherwise requested. This person is the grand average of all persons of [average health], [my] age, [gender], and [peer group], living within [200 miles]. In the chart above, the average person would be at the top center, with +10 being much better than the average person, and -10 indicating danger. Items indicated in the [ ] may be change if desired.

Choose a Specific Question and Proceed to Dowse

Begin with a specific personal question that you would like to experiment with, e.g. gauging the possible side effects of a prescribed medication for yourself. Other areas in which you might ask questions could be related to changes in diet, exercise, sleep, work/life balance, etc.

Dealing with Problematic Findings

If you get a negative or undesirable reading, ask The System if it can and will make corrections. If YES, ask The System to make progressive adjustments, modifications, corrections, or changes towards the highest appropriate positive levels at the appropriate speed.[41]

---

[41] Editor's note: You may also ask how long a requested correction or adjustment is likely to take, or if there is resistance to answering this question, you may investigate further to determine the reasons why an adjustment may be experiencing resistance within your own Subconscious.

Appendix B: Practice Exercises for Beginning Dowsers[42]

The following are suggested practice exercises that may be done as part of a class or on your own to help build your confidence using the dowsing tools.

Black Card/Red Card

Materials needed: One standard deck of playing cards.

Using the deck of playing cards, try to determine if the next card will be red (hearts or diamonds) or black (clubs or spades) using your pendulum or other dowsing tool. Shuffle the cards thoroughly and using the *YES/NO Chart*, ask, "Is the top card black?" and then check your answer. Continue the exercise until the entire deck has been dowsed and keep track of your accurate responses. What you are looking for is a consistent 80% or higher accuracy.

You can increase the challenge by narrowing your question to a specific suit or to only seek face cards (Jack, King, or Queen).

Blue Tape

Materials needed: Blue painter's tape.

Place a three-to-six-foot line of tape on the floor of a hallway or classroom. Ask beginning dowsing students to "find the blue tape" using their dowsing tools. The intention of this exercise is to provide students with what it feels like to

---

[42] Source: American Society of Dowsers "The Foundation Course in Dowsing", 2020 edition.

find a line with their dowsing tool and to follow that line, especially when they can experience visual confirmation that they are doing it right.

Find the Water Bottle

Materials needed: One water bottle and six buckets large enough to hide the bottles completely when inverted.

Place the six buckets around the classroom in random locations leaving at least four feet between them. Underneath one bucket, secretly place the full water bottle. Then ask the students to locate the bucket hiding the water bottle with their dowsing tools. Once all of the students have selected the bucket they believe contains the water bottle, reveal the answer.

Flowing Hoses

Materials needed: To be conducted outdoors. You will need two or three non-transparent water hoses connected to different water spigots, making sure that students cannot see water flowing inside the hoses, which hose is being turned on, nor where the hoses are draining.

Turn on one of the water spigots. Ask the students to find the hose with the flowing water using their dowsing tool. Repeat the exercise by turning off the water spigot that was used and starting again. Do this at least three times. You may use the same spigot more than once.

Hidden Treasure

Materials needed: Any number of identical bags that are large enough to obscure whatever is hidden inside. Different objects that are roughly the same size and shape. Suggestions include:

- An envelope containing a personal note.
- Paper money (any denomination will do).
- A photograph of an animal.
- A greeting card.
- An envelope containing a coin, key, or some other metallic object.

Place a different object in each bag and shuffle the bags so that nobody knows what is inside any one bag. Tell each student what they are looking for, or make a visible list and inform them that one of the objects is hidden in each bag. For the last bag, add the previous bags and shuffle the bags around. Label them by number, with the answer being a numbered bag. After each student has had a chance to do so, reveal the results to the group.

Monte Carlo

Materials needed: Three-to-five opaque drinking cups, preferably 16-24 oz each. Different colored balls that are small enough to fit completely under each cup. You may also substitute different small plush toys or pet toys for the balls.

While the class watches, place a different object under each cup and mix the cups like street performer on the streets of Monte Carlo. Then ask your students to identify what is under each cup using their dowsing tool. When all students (or in a large class, a specific number) have answered, remove the cup to check for their accuracy.

Hide and Seek

Materials needed: Two objects that are identical but not a "common" object. Examples include:
- A pair of teething keys for babies
- A pair of small brightly colored plush toys

The instructor will hide one of the objects in a room. When it is time to "seek", the instructor will show the object's "twin" to the class and ask students to find the object with their dowsing tools. This game will help students develop question-asking skills.

Is this beneficial for me?

Materials needed: Any number of small identical bottles. Wrap each bottle with blue painter's tape and label each with a number or letter. Fill each bottle with various liquids, some that are beneficial, some that are not and seal the bottles so they cannot be opened, making a list, which the instructor has, of the contents in each labeled bottle. Contents examples might include:
- Filtered or spring water.
- Dish/laundry detergent
- Saline or salt solution
- Mouthwash
- Vitamin C solution
- Bleach

Ask the students to dowse the question, "Are the contents of this bottle good for me to drink?" and have each student record their results.

This same exercise can use paper lunch bags containing various food and non-food items where the students will be unable to use anything other than dowsing (e.g. sight, sound, taste, smell, weight, feel, etc.) to determine what is inside the bag.

Note: There could be some individual differences caused by food allergies or intolerances, so it might be fun to ask follow-up questions using your dowsing tool when outliers occur, especially if the student was unaware that they had an intolerance to a particular food item!

Appendix C: Brief History of Dowsing[43]

Dowsing is as old as mankind. The act of dowsing involves searching for something using a tool, such as a twig, rod, or pendulum as an indicator.

Ancient Egyptians and Babylonians would dowse with split reeds. Chinese Emperor Kwang Sung (c 2200 BCE) was a known dowser. The use of dowsing by early Jews is recorded in the Old Testament. Moses used a dowsing device referred to as "the Rod" to locate and bring forth water.

Alfred the Great, king of the Anglo-Saxons from 848-899 CE was called "The Truth Teller" because he was a dowser. Alfred's greatest victory was defeating the Viking advance at the battle of Edington in 878 CE. "The Alfred Jewel" (discovered in 1693) is an intricate piece of Anglo-Saxon jewelry that depicts a man holding two wooden rods with the jewel affixed to the top, much like a bobber or Y-Rod. Similar, but less intricate jewels from the same period were also discovered in similar sites across what would have been Alfred's kingdom, which suggests that dowsing was a common practice during his reign.[44]

During the Middle Ages and throughout the Spanish Inquisition, dowsing was associated with witchcraft and the occult, which forced many dowsers to practice their craft in secret.

The earliest printed illustration of a dowser in action comes from *De Re Metallica (On the Nature of Metals or Minerals)* by Georgius Agricola. The book shows early metallurgists searching for veins of metal in the earth using forked twigs.

---

[43] Source: American Society of Dowsers "The Foundation Course in Dowsing", 2020 edition.
[44] Source: Ashmolean Museum, Oxford.

Letter to Robin

In 1853, the Catholic Church reversed its backing of the dowsing treatise, *La Phsique Occulte, ou Traité de la Baguette Divinatoire* (subtitle: Occult Physics, or Treatise on the Divine Wand and its Utility for Discovering Water Springs, Minerals, Hidden Treasures, Thieves & Fugitive Murderers, with principles that explain the darkest phenomena of nature). It then declared that the reason dowsing worked was because the devil himself pulled and twisted the dowsing rod to give accurate results. This resulted in further persecution of dowsers in European communities and led to superstitions about dowsing in general that continue to this day.

20th Century French priest, Abbe Mermet, proved his belief that, if it was possible to divine the location and state of an underground stream, it should be equally possible to use dowsing to learn about the human bloodstream. He coined the word, radiesthesia to refer to the use of dowsing in medicine.[45]

The American Society of Dowsers, Inc., (ASD) was founded and incorporated in 1961 in the state of Vermont as a scientific and educational non-profit organization. The ASD currently maintains its headquarters and bookstore in Danville, VT.

The ASD's mission is "to support, encourage, and promote dowsing and dowsers in a manner consistent with the highest standards of personal integrity and behavior; to provide dowsing education and training to dowsers and non-dowsers alike to bring them to a level of proficiency they are comfortable with, to promote and foster communication and fellowship among all persons in any way interested in dowsing."

---

[45] Sources:
Comment j'opère (Paris, 1935)
Emmart, Barney D. "All Purpose Dowsing". *The Atlantic*. July 1952.

Walt Woods

Today, ASD has chapters and members from every state, territory and from around the world. Its annual National Conference and Convention draws hundreds of individuals interested in teaching and learning about all of the dimensions of energy and fields of dowsing. Regional conferences are held throughout the USA, especially on the West Coast and Southwest United States, and local chapters host a variety of dowsing events on a regular basis.

ASD members have been consulted by the US Government, states, and private businesses on issues including water, land mines, lost persons and objects, minerals and other natural resources. Members of ASD have also served individuals worldwide on personal issues, water wells, farming, animals, home and property clearing, and health concerns.

From whatever viewpoint, scientific or psychic phenomenon, started by miners looking for metals, developed by civil engineers looking for water sources, condemned by the Church as evil, used by armies and medical personnel worldwide to save lives – dowsing is a phenomenon in itself that has many applications far and above those from which it first started.

Appendix D
Student and ASD Testimonials
About Walt Woods

"Walt Woods' simple book was my introduction to dowsing when I went to my first American Society of Dowsers (ASD) convention in 1984. Walt was a schoolteacher, and his book is a good first textbook for those who wish to learn dowsing." - Michael O. Patterson

"Walt Woods was my mentor. He was always willing to give of his time for me and for others. His booklet, *Letter to Robin*, was so good that I would purchase them by the box and hand them out. He was one of the best dowsers and human beings I have ever known." - Michael Hoefler, Dowser and Energy Worker

"Like many others, *Letter to Robin* was my introduction to dowsing - clear and concise. It gave me the dowsing skills to be able to help others. I had the pleasure of meeting Walt Woods in a Vermont class, so was doubly blessed by his knowledge and expertise. - Mary McGrane

I first met Walt at the 1997 ASD Convention in Vermont, where, as a relatively inexperienced dowser I heard about *Letter to Robin*. Unfortunately, I had already made other Convention purchases which I believed had used up my duty-free limit for returning to Canada. When I attended the ORI Winter School in Arkansas where Walt was presenting new scientific information related to dowsing, I asked via pendulum if I should buy *Letter to Robin* at the book display. I was surprised to get a NO. Several times during the school, I repeated the dowsing question, and kept on getting a NO response. What could that mean? As the school was ending, I finally got my answer. My roommate, by then also a good friend, presented me with a gift copy as a souvenir of our time together!

Both Walt and I ended up staying overnight to catch morning flights home. He agreed to autograph my copy at breakfast time. Since then, *Letter to Robin* has been part of my dowsing reference library, and I have encouraged many to download the pdf. Thank you, ASD, for publishing it officially, along with other guidelines and articles that Walt developed. Today's new dowsers will gain so many helpful ideas on developing their skills and establishing new Programs that will expand dowsing's applications to new fields of knowledge.

-Joan Nathanson, an enthusiastic Canadian daily dowser

Appendix E
Articles Written by Walt Woods
and Mardi Gieseler

The End of AIDS?[46]

BY WALTER WOODS AND MARDI GIESELER

At the Canadian Society of Questors' Conference in 100-Mile House the keynote speaker was a Professor of Geography at the University of Victoria. Dr. Harold Foster gave one of the most astounding lectures we have heard in a long time. He is a medical geographer who looks geographically where diseases occur, or do not occur, and studies the reasons why.

AIDS: A Nutritional Disease

In his research, Dr. Foster noted that AIDS is epidemic in most sub-Saharan African countries except one, Senegal. Why would Senegal have such a low AIDS rate (1-2%) when in all of the surrounding countries it is so high, sometimes in excess of 25+ % of the population? After many years of research, Dr. Foster has evidence that a deficiency of the trace-mineral selenium and

---

[46] Source: https://www.ptangels.com/pdf/Cure.pdf (n.d.)

167

three essential amino acids can cause all of the symptoms of AIDS, with or without the HIV virus. In Africa, only Senegal has abundant selenium in the soil and water and adequate nutrition (amino acids).

Although these nutrients are not a cure for HIV infection, research studies found that high doses of selenium and the three essential amino acids (cysteine, glutamine, and tryptophan) given to AIDS patients eliminated most of the AIDS symptoms, sometimes in as little as two or three weeks, and allowing the patient to return to work in as little as one month.

Dr. Foster now has ongoing studies in Uganda and Zambia to study the effects of selenium and these three amino acids on large numbers of AIDS patients. Recently Dr. Foster wrote about a double-blind clinical study; "The news from the Ugandan 300 patient trial is very good. Many are recovering rapidly."

(Personal communication, March 2006: 99% of the AIDS patients in the African research trials are responding well to the supplements of selenium and amino acids.)

1

Why Does HIV Infection Become AIDS?

Selenium and the three amino acids are necessary for the body to produce glutathione peroxidase, which is essential for the human immune system to be healthy and is also important for many other vital body functions. Research indicates that the HIV virus needs selenium and the three amino acids in order to replicate. The HIV virus is very good at robbing these vital nutrients from the human body it has infected, leaving the body malnourished. Thus, infection with HIV leaves the human body with a depressed immune system which is unable to fight off the opportunistic diseases which characterize AIDS.

Other Diseases

HIV I and II are not the only viruses that rob these nutrients from the human body. The viruses of Hepatitis A, B, and C, Coxsackie B (thought to be responsible for 1/4 of heart attacks), and other viruses (which encode for a glutathione peroxidase) leave the human body depleted of the necessary nutrients to keep the immune system healthy and functional. Selenium and the three amino acids are also implicated in many cancers, thyroid malfunction, senility, and depression. Some researchers have estimated that as many as 1/3 of the patients in hospitals for depression are simply selenium deficient.

In the 1970's and 80's before many of us had even heard of HIV/AIDS, researchers were studying the relationship of selenium deficiency to cancer. Dr. Foster noted that Senegal, the African country with such high levels of selenium and low rates of HIV/AIDS infection, also has the lowest rate of cancer on earth.

The Disease Belt

In China, there is a large area from the northeast to the southwest that is called the "Disease Belt" where the Hepatitis, Coxsackie B, and AIDS are all on the rise. The Chinese government added selenium supplements to the soils, table salt, and animal feed stocks, and subsequently found a significant reduction in these diseases. For example, in one study of 21,000 people given selenium in their table salt, the hepatitis infection rate dropped more than 50%.

2

Selenium Bioavailability

We get our necessary amount of selenium from the foods that we eat or from supplementation. Food grown on selenium-deficient soil, and animals fed selenium-deficient food-stocks are contributing to a decrease in selenium in the food chain.

Atmospheric pollution in the rainfall, such as mercury and sulfur, combine with selenium to form insoluble compounds which make selenium unavailable to plants and animals.

In recent years acid rain changed the pH of the soil, decreasing the bioavailability of selenium. Soil acidification lowers the abundance of selenium in the global food chain, which may have contributed to the rapid rise of cancers and HIV/AIDS.

Toxic Levels of Selenium

Many people think that selenium is highly toxic. While an overdose is possible, a healthy person needs about 200 mcg/day; however, an HIV infected individual may need 10 times that amount for a while to bring selenium to a healthy level. The first indications of toxicity are garlic breath and yellow fingernails which occur in a sensitive person at about 1000 mcg/day.

We have tried to make a very complicated subject readable for most everyone. We have only touched the tip of the iceberg concerning the health effects of selenium and the three amino acids, as well as, the environmental reasons why selenium is being depleted worldwide. If you are interested in more information, there are many sources on the Internet.

Dowsing

It is important to dowse your own nutrition every day and bring it to optimum for your body. Almost all diseases are nutritionally based either primarily or secondarily. If you wish to know more about, see www.lettertorobin.org or Reference: "Health and Nutrition Secrets that can save your life", Russell Blaylock, M.D., Health Press 2006.

3

More Information

Dr. Foster has a web site where three of his books are available to buy or free to download. Look at www.hdfoster.com for "What Really Causes AIDS,"" What Really Causes Alzheimer's," and "What Really Causes Schizophrenia.". He is now working on a book which will probably be out in 2007, "What Really Causes Multiple Sclerosis."

Cell Communication[47]

BY WALT WOODS AND MARDI GIESELER

Have you ever thought about talking to your cells? There is scientific evidence that we (our thoughts) are in direct communication with all of our cells, even if they are separated from our bodies.

The Backster Effect: Cleve Backster, world renowned polygraph expert, teacher, and director of the Backster Research Foundation started working with bio-communication in the 60's. His first experiments demonstrated that plants respond to their care-giver's thoughts. The printout on a polygraph machine attached to a plant leaf showed a strong fear reaction when Backster thought about going to another room to get a match to burn a leaf.

For the last 38 years Cleve has continued to research bio-communication with all kinds of plants, living foods, and human cells demonstrating that we are in thought communication with living things.

One fascinating experiment, which may have clues on how are our "healing talents" operate, involves our ability to communicate with our white blood cells.

The Experiments: An experimental subject washes out his/her mouth with a saline solution in order to collect oral leukocytes (white blood cells which reside in the lining of the mouth). The leukocytes, which belong to the immune

---

[47] Source: https://www.ptangels.com/pdf/cellcommunicationarticle.pdf (n.d.)

system, are then concentrated in a test tube by centrifuging. Two very small gold electrodes are placed into the group of cells in the test tube.

The electrodes are attached to an amplifier and a voltmeter connected to a graph recorder to document any electrical signal from the cells. (No electricity is passed through the cells; only the signal produced by the cells is recorded.)

The experimental subject then leaves the laboratory to go many miles away from his/her cells. The distances have been up to hundreds of miles away from their cells in the laboratory.

The Results: Any strong emotional or physical stimulus to the subject, no matter how far they are away from their cells in the laboratory, is sensed by the cells which then generate voltages which are recorded on a graph. Our cells respond to whatever is happening to us.

Dr. Brian O'Leary, an astronaut and author of a book called *The Quest for Reality* (O'Leary 1989), was one of Cleve Backster's experimental research subjects testing leukocyte responses. O'Leary is quoted; "This one experiment proved to me as a skeptical scientist that we could measure force fields of communication in consciousness that defy the known laws of physics."

Hundreds of times this experiment has been repeated at Backster's Research laboratory demonstrating our ability to affect the immune system.

Cleve Backster's new book describing his years of experiments with bio-communication has just been published. It is an easy-to-read book written in non-scientific language with many illustrations.

Walt Woods

Primary Perception, Biocommunication with Plants, Living Foods, and Human Cells.
By Cleve Backster

For more information see- www.primaryperception.com Reprinted with permission from authors and the Ozark Research Institute Journal.

Memorial Tributes to Walt Woods[48]

Zuerrnnovahh-Starr Livingstone

Canadian Society of Questers

Walt Woods, the master dowser who wrote *A Letter to Robin* to teach a young woman how to dowse, has been the doorway for many to learning how to use this powerful tool. I saw him at two Questers' conferences and believe he taught at earlier conferences.

He had an easy gentle manner in the way he presented Beginner and Intermediate Dowsing. He would say dowsers are the most powerful people in the world in a way that rang true but for new students a challenge to their beliefs. He dared people to work with their pendulums, L-rods and willow sticks.

He would tell stories about his experiences intermixed with the protocols he used. He used dowsing to activate dormant genes. One of his most famous activations was of the vitamin C gene. He did that for everybody in his classes and in fact made the activation universal. He reasoned if most mammals could

---

[48] Published with permission by the authors

produce their own vitamin C and never experienced scurvy why should not humans be able to do the same? The operation took a few minutes with a pendulum and most people did not notice any change. To my knowledge nobody who attended his classes suffered scurvy…in fact I have heard very little about scurvy in any news broadcasts from anywhere in the world. Maybe Walt Woods cured that deficiency disease once and for all.

He was also working on age regression personally by shutting down the genes related to aging. At age 85 he looked like he was in his late 60s. He had a lot of vitality. He was planning on living to age 120 and he was doing his utmost on a daily dowse for himself and others. He died "young".

One of the most interesting bits of knowledge he brought up was the electro-encephalogram testing done on him and other master dowsers. Experienced meditators are able to shift from waking state Beta brain wave activity to Alpha deep relaxation states. In sleep the brain initially operates in Delta frequency and in deep sleep it is in Theta where rapid eye movement occurs. Wired to the EEG Walt Woods was in all four frequencies at the same time while dowsing. The operator of the EEG was startled and looked at Walt. Walt asked him if there was a problem. The operator of the EEG said Walt should be unconscious. Other master dowsers had the same results.

I have thought about these strange EEG readings and now believe "dowsers are the most powerful people in the world."

Letter to Robin

Ken Adachi[49]

Editor of Educate Yourself: The Freedom of Knowledge, The Power of Thought

I received a phone call this morning from an old friend, Pat, who told me that Walt Woods had passed away. He was 85 years old. His wife, Madi, reported that Walt died a little after midnight in the early morning hours of August 12, 2011

Walt had recently been hospitalized in northern California. Friends of Walt's reported that they had lunch with him at his hospital location on August 11, just 12 hours or so prior to his passing.

In addition to Walt's many positions held as a master dowser, including current president of the Sierra Dowsers Chapter, Walt was also Founder and First President of the Subtle Energy Research Institute (SERI) http://seri-worldwide.org/

Walt had been a teacher in radiobiology for many years prior to his 'retirement' and his new career as dowsing seminar leader.

I attended many master classes and workshops with Walt Woods. He was a wonderful and inspiring human being. He created enthusiasm and joy in all he met and talked to. As a teacher, he could hold his class spellbound with a well-

---

[49] Source: https://educate-yourself.org/lte/waltwoodspasses13aug11.shtml (August, 2011)

balanced mix of amazing information coupled with wit, humor, and cartoon jokes. I loved the guy. He's the sort of teacher that everyone should encounter in high school, college, and beyond.

His ability as a dowser was uncanny. He could derive the answer to just about any question posed if you frame the question correctly-and that's exactly what Walt taught you in his dowsing seminars. Of course, many people know of the name Walt Woods from his wonderful little booklet called A Letter to Robin, which is still available on the Products page. .

The extraordinary knowledge freely shared by Walt Woods will remain with me, and all of his student, forever. I learned so much from him about metaphysics, science, and the workings of the spirit realm. He was like an Arthur C. Clark, Lopsang Rampa, and Yogananda character rolled into one unassuming and modest mannered man, but a very powerful individual and great in the ways that count.

He will be sorely missed on the earthly plane, but I -and everyone who knew him- know full well that he will be continuing his work as a gifted teacher and inspirational model for many other souls who may encounter his wonderful presence on different planes of existence.

God Bless you Walt, you did a magnificent job to help so many to see the Light and the true path to follow in life.

Letter to Robin

About Walt Woods

Born June 28, 1926, in Vacaville, CA, Walter H. Woods Jr. passed away August 12, 2011 from an unexpected heart condition.

Walt graduated from Oroville High School, enlisted in the Air Force during WWII, attained his bachelor's degree from Chico State University, earned a master's degree in teaching, and was Director of the X-ray Technology Program at Yuba College for twenty years.

Walt Woods

Walt was a polymath and had an unquenchable thirst for learning and exploring. He was a consummate sailor and a Past President of Lake Oroville Yacht Club. He was a passionate life-long dowser, Past President and Trustee of The American Society of Dowsers, and President of the Sierra Dowsers of Sacramento.

Walt lectured and taught throughout the United States and Canada on various subjects. He was ever expanding into a sustainable lifestyle and fostered an interest in green technology. A defining thread throughout his life was his optimistic concern with the plight of humanity and his genuine desire to help people.

Walt was always teaching, both inside and outside of the classroom. He expanded minds and provided guidance through what he did, as much as what he said. He touched countless lives and will be lovingly remembered by friends all over the world.[50]

---

[50] Source: https://www.legacy.com/us/obituaries/chicoer/name/walter-woods-obituary?id=20347878

Acknowledgments

This book in its current form would not have been possible without the many hours of dedication by the following people.

Nina Gee
(Editor, cover design, illustrations, initial layout and design)
www.ninagee.com

William Gee
(Editor, project leader, layout and design)
www.vitalbioenergetics.com

Joan Nathanson
(Copy editor, former editor of *The American Dowser*, the quarterly journal of the
American Society of Dowsers)

Paul Flipse
(Copy editor, current editor of *The American Dowser*)

Index

Printed in Great Britain
by Amazon

59385724R00104